EXILE IN GUYVILLE

EXILE IN GUYVILLE

How a Punk-Rock Redneck Faggot Texan
Moved to West Hollywood and Refused
to Be Shiny and Happy

DAVE WHITE

NEW YORK

AUTHOR'S NOTE: Some of the events described happened as related, others were expanded and changed. Some of the individuals portrayed are composites of more than one person and many names and identifying characteristics have been changed as well.

Manufactured in the United States of America.
This trade paperback original is published by Alyson Books,
P.O. Box 1253, Old Chelsea Station, New York, NY 100113-1251.

Distribution in the United Kingdom by Turnaround Publisher Services Ltd., Unit 3 Olympia Trading Estate, Coburg Road, Wood Green,
London N22 6TZ England.

Library of Congress Cataloging-in-Publication Data has been applied for.

First Edition April 2006

06 07 08 09 **a** 10 9 8 7 6 5 4 3 2 1

ISBN 1-55583-932-0
ISBN 978-1-55583-932-1
Cover Design by Michelle Thompson
Book Design by Victor Mingovits

THANKS TO...

EDITORS WHO GAVE ME WORK:
Gabriel Goldberg, Laurie Pike, Lew Harris, David Ciminelli, Parker Ray, Mikel Wadewitz, LD Beghtol, Laurie Ochoa, Anne Stockwell, Bruce Steele, J. R. Griffin, Mike Wolf, Darren Frei

ALYSON DUDES:
Nick Street, Joe Pittman

MY FAMILY:
Matt and Jill White, Mark and Bambi White, Tim and Rebecca White, Joanna Potter

PANCAKE PALS:
Dennis Hensley, Mark Salzberg, Terence McFarland, Dennis Smeal, Kate Smeal, Bryan Fuller, Tom Ford, Charlotte Del Rose, Tony Tripoli, Tom Walsh, the Vegans and the Bears, Erin Quill, Rick Andreoli, Laura Kim, Betty Kim, Margy Rochlin, Robert Abele, Dave Cobb, Jason Havard, Sean Abley, Vincent Lopez, Maryam Akhavizadeh, Anderson Jones

This book is all Alonso Duralde's fault.

BEFORE - 1999

I REALLY HOPE you haven't picked up this book thinking it's going to help you learn something about humanity or life or whatever. If that were the case, it would have tips or hints or something, maybe even one helpful bit of advice about how to make over your life with ease and grace, or, as in my case, make a cross-country move from a beloved hometown to a gay ghetto in a big city and fit in and not be constantly mortified. But it doesn't.

This book is simply the one-year diary of a man who grew up in a nomadic, unstable family, and who as an adult decided to make a stubborn fetish out of staying put. Then that man found himself uprooted in the middle of his life and dumped, panting and sweating, into an unfamiliar environment. That's when he sat and complained about it, all the while stuffing his face with doughnuts.

In 1997, my boyfriend of two years decided he wanted to return from our then home of Dallas, Texas, to his native Los Angeles. I wished him luck and had private, excellent thoughts about how this meant that I would finally have space to stretch out in bed. It's a queen-size but we're not skinny people.

In 1998, my boyfriend of three years decided he wanted to return from our then home of Dallas, Texas, to his native Los Angeles. He had spent the remainder of 1997 brainwashing me into a sort of hostage state, so I was a little more receptive to the idea. It would have been a lot fucking cooler if he'd used his newfound mind-control powers over me to tart me up in an SLA T-shirt with a seven-headed snake on the front and taken me out on a few bank heists.

In 1999, my boyfriend of four years decided he wanted to return from our then home of Dallas, Texas, to his native Los Angeles. This time we actually drove across four states to West Hollywood. Somewhere in western New Mexico, as the U-Haul rumbled nearer and nearer to our final resting place, I started panicking and didn't stop for another year. I can't say why I freaked out exactly, but it seemed like the right thing to do at the time.

The freak-outs were documented. Weekly diaries in e-mail form went out, at first, to family and friends in other states. As time went on, strangers began e-mailing me, asking to be added to my mailing list. I couldn't understand why people who didn't know me were finding entertainment value in my anxiety attacks and disgruntled rants about living in Los Angeles. But they did, and the mailing list grew. It turned out that people were forwarding the diaries on to friends, who in turn shared them with co-workers, who would then forward them on to other friends. I received what can only be described as scary "fan" mail about diary entries that were frequently about nothing more than descriptions of people who stood in line in front of me at the supermarket.

Eventually, the diaries became a blog called "Dave White Knows" and, in 2003, became a monthly column in *Instinct* magazine called "Exile in Guyville." That column focused on a fairly small-scale incident each month, an incident that was then blown totally out of proportion by me, conniption-fitted-over, then used as evidence in my case for moving back home to Texas. That column also inspired the first writer-centered hate mail in the history of *Instinct*. The readers who disliked it, to a man, requested more fashion and skin-care product features to replace it.

P.S. Listen to some Slayer while you read this book. It'll make it way better.

1

DENIAL
July & August

EVIL

A THING THAT sucks about West Hollywood: Deadbeat tenants have rights. Don't misunderstand. I'm all about tenants having rights and power to the people and all that, just as long as those tenants are not wickedly working the system because they're selfish, lazy bastards who then get in my way. I like *my* way, the way I've spent months planning and making meticulous to-do lists for, to be made smooth and clear of asshole-constructed obstacles. That's what I like.

My boyfriend is a handsome, chunky, four-eyed guy who, for the purposes of this story, will henceforth be known as Morocco Mole. He chose this secret identity a long time ago when I decided to publish a sort of too-cute punk-rockish zine about our lives. His protest against my using his real name in that failed attempt at underground literary notoriety went something like, "I prefer to slink through the shadows, undetected, like Diabolik." Or else it was, "Keep me out of your fucktarded zine." I forget which.

He drives a U-Haul up to our new apartment in West Hollywood on July 1, 1999. It's a mid-century, two-story building. It's got elements of those Googie diners you see in books about architecture from the period. It's on a pretty, green, tree-lined residential street that sits in the middle of the urban belching contest of Santa Monica Boulevard and Sunset Boulevard. The famous Chateau Marmont, the hotel where celebrities like to go to be interviewed by entertainment journalists, gang-banged by high-priced, triple-teaming escorts and sometimes overdosed and left to die, sits at the top of our street. And we've meandered our way through five states for the past three days to get here. We're both exhausted and our butts have been sticking to the U-Haul seats since Flagstaff. We have, however, the assurance that upon arrival we will be ushered right into our new home.

This is not the case.

A good dozen friends, ones that Morocco left behind the first time, have shown up to help us unload the truck. Then Landlady Elaine pulls up in her Lexus to tell us that the old tenants have not left yet, that the escrow on their new home has not closed, that they have decided not to leave until that happens ("they say maybe on the seventh of July"), and that legally she can do nothing about it. It could take months to evict them if they decide to squat in the apartment for which we have already paid two months' rent. Elaine can't even give us a key until these people decide to leave. My exhaustion seizes this opportunity to turn to anger.

Normally I'm pretty patient. No, make that totally patient. I am the Job of Dallas, Texas. I was a middle-school teacher for eight years, employment that will jackhammer patience into you if you don't come with it standard. I managed roomfuls of pre-literate kids, fourteen-year-old Sudanese genocide refugees who'd never been in a school before and wondered why those bells rang every fifty minutes. But that was different. Those were shell-shocked war waifs adjusting to a new country. These folks, on the other hand, were adults who had somehow managed to pony up the cash to buy a house in Los Angeles, a place I will come to learn is one of the most out-of-control real-estate markets in the country, but who were too poor to go get a hotel until their fucking escrow closed. I decide that these pricks need me to explain to them that they're being pricks. I'm already on edge from the drive into town on freeways I think I'll be avoiding for my entire stay here, nervous about meeting so many of Morocco Mole's California people all at once, and sopping wet from the heat, which I was promised was of a very temperate quality in this seaside city but in fact is totally not behaving like the tourist brochure said it would. So I choose this moment to have a psychotic "Hulk Smash!" episode.

It's an impressive one. I scream and rant and use all the bad swears I know. I do this in front of Morocco's backing-away-slowly friends and in front of our new neighbors. They've come outside to see what the fuss is all about and who is that man who keeps bellowing "Cocksuckers!" and "Motherfuckers!" over and over. But I don't care. In fact, I'm thinking it's probably a good move. Establish craziness right out of the box and no one will bother me again. I go up to our door and knock loudly. A tussle awaits these people, or, at least, the use of my strict disciplinarian teacher voice to make them obey me awaits them. There's no answer. I make sure to give the door a good kick before stomping back down the stairs. The fact that I'm kicking and potentially damaging my own future door is lost in my brain's tornado of justice-delayed-hate-fury.

But this moment isn't strictly about me having a detonating anger management issue. It's also about my lifelong knowledge that I'm destined to live in a box under a bridge with winos. I did time in trailer parks and other shitty dwellings as a kid—also with winos, some of them related to me—so I've come to suspect that squalor is always plotting to reach up and grab me without warning. That means that right now I'm wondering how we'll take turns sleeping in the U-Haul truck tonight so that we're not brutally murdered by the kind of U-Haul robbers you always hear about sneaking into Motel 6 parking lots under cover of darkness, making off with families' entire lives, stabbing them for kicks.

To defuse my explosion, Morocco's friend Laura, who works as a movie publicist, invites us to stay in the spare bedroom of her house until the dispute is settled. Her sister Betty, who lives with her, agrees with that idea and asks if either of us has a problem with dogs. Morocco shoots me a concerned glance, then starts in on how I'm allergic to all things that live and grow on Earth, including adorable dogs. But I quickly break in with the save. "I have no problems!" I shout, knowing better than to wreck a good thing by being all gay about pet dander.

The next day, after a deeply fatigued sleep, I call the lingering tenants of my apartment. God, I used to think squatting was so punk rock. Here's the entire transcript of that conversation:

Horrible Excuse for a Human Being: Hello?

Me: Hello. We're the people who were supposed to move in yesterday. We need to move our stuff into the apartment so that we can return the U-Haul. Otherwise we have to keep paying for it. We've already paid our deposit and our first and last months' rent on that apartment you're still occupying, so we have to put our stuff inside it. When will you be home next so that we can come back and do that?

Horrible Excuse for a Human Being: We're not finished moving our own stuff into the house yet so there's really no room for—

Me: Look, I need one room of that apartment and all or most of our stuff will fit in it. This has to happen because we have to return the U-Haul. Will tomorrow afternoon work for you?

Horrible Excuse for a Human Being: Uh…sure.

The next day we return to the apartment to unload the truck. I'm rested and I've refilled my prescription of calm-the-fuck-down pills. The three not-going-anywhere-soon-enough-ers, whom we've decided to call the Evil Fuckers, are waiting for us. As the same bunch of Morocco's friends re-arrive to help, I announce the number-one rule of the day: No one is to speak to the Evil Fuckers. If spoken to by the Evil Fuckers, simply glare at them. A hole-in-skull-boring-so-as-to-make-blood-spurt-from-it stare. Grunting's okay.

Thirty minutes in, I learn that one of the Evil Fuckers has dared to speak to one of my box-lugging gang. "That cow said, 'Sorry for the misunderstanding,'" says Betty, whose deadpan delivery sends chills down my spine. "But I just gave her the stare. No blood spurted, though." Not skipping a beat, she continues, "Wow! I love this Eames chair!" These friends of Morocco's are beautiful people. I'm going to like them. But even so, I'm troubled by visions of strangers oc-cupying my new home, self-absorbed creeps who can't be trusted to behave decently, doing terrible things to all our precious stuff: stealing it, peeing on it, worse.

Four hours of box-stacking, chair-admiring, icy-staring and truck-returning later, we're back at Laura and Betty's house. Laura barbecues ribs in the backyard and we stuff ourselves. And though it's only seven o'clock, I'm ready for bed. I shower the crud off me, get into pajamas, and pick up a book of essays by the late Cookie Mueller that I've retrieved from the box of books marked "NON-FICTION ANTHOLOGIES." I'm that organized. Cookie wasn't. She starred in lots of early John Waters movies and was the kind of adventurer that I am not, a woman who, when confronted by life's problems, would incite a party, jump up on a table, and dance with a bottle of champagne in her hand, daring the bad shit to knock her off it. I'm as worn out and anxiety-ridden—the U-Haul place is closed so that's one more day of dollars down the drain—as I've been in quite a while, so reading her is like being vicariously courageous.

Eventually we move in. Nine days later. Nine days that felt like sitting in coach as the plane endlessly circled an iced-in airport, waiting for permission to land or crash trying. Morocco and I have accomplished very little in that time besides getting on each other's nerves. But now it's time. We drive up to the apartment and I walk upstairs to the door. I knock. The door opens and I greet the Queen of the Evil Fuckers as she packs up her own stuff. She's had nine days to get it together and she's still boxing her trinkets. She says, "We're leaving today, but is it necessary for you to be here while we pack up?"

"Yes," I say. "My asthma inhaler's refill canister is in one of those boxes and I have to find it now. My last one ran out yesterday."

She stares at me for a second. "I have *asthma,*" I say with extra emphasis.

I don't have asthma. But what I do have are superior haunting skills that I will use on them until they break, their stubborn wills shattered by victorious me. I have vowed to make them as miserable as they've been making us. To that end, I've called their house every day, leaving messages like,

"When are you leaving my apartment?" Subtlety is for other people. Queen of the Evil Fuckers sighs, blows a cloud of carbon monoxide from her cigarette in my direction, and lets me in.

Their revenge? To leave behind a giant, amber, smoked-Plexiglas column, function unknown. There's still a sticker on the bottom of the thing that reads, "HANDCRAFTED FROM 100% ACRYLIC." In another room they've left a broken exercise bike. I like to think that she used that bike once while watching a *Believercise for Bicycles* tape on her top-loading VCR. I like to imagine her crappy Daewoo TV on top of that smoked-Plexiglas column. I like to imagine the exercise bike breaking down the week after the Christmas her husband gave it to her as a not-subtle hint that she's getting too fat for him to fuck, and that she was secretly happy when it fell apart because she'd never even asked for an exercise bike, it was just him doling out hints about her lumpy ass, and fuck him anyway because California has community-property laws and she'll get to keep that new house they're moving into. How's he gonna like *that*. I like to think she took up smoking after the bike broke, just to spite him some more.

I open up a box of CDs marked "A–C" and pick at random.

Boris, the sludgy Japanese doom-metal band: rejected. Too jarring.

Cat Power, the sleepy, one-lady arty folk band: rejected. Too much emotionally sensitive listening required.

Selected CD = Autechre. Bloopy but not intrusive. Morocco heads to the back bedroom to start hooking up the computer and I begin unpacking books. My low-key obsessive-compulsive tendencies want me to locate "FICTION: A–C" but it's nowhere to be found right now. So I head for the boxes marked "FICTION: D–F," and try to remember which circle Dante assigned to the rude and selfish. Sitting on the floor, surrounded by stacks, I learn that the closest class of bad people to the Evil Fuckers are the Spenders and Hoarders. This is a fairly accurate fit, since they spent more time than they were supposed to in *our apartment* and hoarded the square footage of *our apartment* longer than they had a right to do so. Dante gave them over to the fourth ring of fire. Hope they repent soon.

Five hours later, we're buried in boxes. We're hot, sweaty, hungry, and having an argument. And yet, for some reason, Morocco Mole still decides that this is a good time for us to walk down the street to West Hollywood City Hall to register as domestic partners. "No way," I say.

"Yes way," counters Morocco. "We have to do this today. It's Friday. Monday I begin job-hunting and if I get one that recognizes domestic partnerships when it comes to health insurance then you'll get to be on my policy. If we don't do this then all your teeth will fall out because last time I checked dentists no longer take impressive indie-rock cred as payment. Unless you *want* to be like Shane MacGowan."

"Fuck," I agree.

When we enter West Hollywood City Hall, a block away from the new apartment, however, we're still in the middle of a prior argument that was about nothing in particular and talks have broken down. It's merely a symptom of my current round-the-clock state of rage, really. It'll end as soon as one of us apologizes for being an ass—most likely me, since I'm the one who's all bent out of shape about every single thing that's happened since we arrived in this hellmouth of a city.

We sign the forms, pay the processing fee, and go sit down. Ten minutes later a man comes out with a paper that declares us as legal as two faggots can get outside the Netherlands. The guy says, excitedly, "I now pronounce you domestic partners!" and suddenly from behind we hear several city employees shriek, "Whoooo!" Then they bombard us with confetti. I could not be less amused. I am fighting with my domestic partner and these dizzy queens are throwing shit in my hair. I decide right there that I officially hate West Hollywood. I stomp out the door, muttering, "This is the happiest day of my life."

Other stuff that happens:

1. I have my first celebrity sighting since becoming a West Hollywood resident: an unshaven, haggard Judd Nelson. Recently canned from "Suddenly Susan," he's tossing a cigarette butt into traffic before entering a gym. Have a good workout, you fuckin' nicotine-fingered litterbug.

2. I have my first burger at a chain called In-N-Out and it's so delicious I think I might cry. It's the first good thing to happen to me here. But why is John 3:16 stamped on the bottom of my root beer cup?

ANGRY

MY NEW NEIGHBORHOOD:

Queens = 65 percent.

Cranky seventy-year-old Russians who give you the evil eye when you walk past them on the sidewalk = 20 percent.

Blonde chicks with big round hard fakeys. The kind of women who think Jennifer Aniston just got lucky = 10 percent.

Miscellaneous cool kids, the homeless, Deuce Bigalows, broke-down druggies, and actual crazy people = 5 percent.

That equals 100 percent not like Texas. I'm already homesick.

Repping for the crazy people is an almost-elderly neighbor—but the kind who wears really tight appliquéd jeans anyway and lots of makeup—all cranked up about her underground parking space. She makes me aware of this by leaving a terse note on one of our cars. The note reads: "This is my space. Do not park here."

So I knock on her door.

"Hi, we just moved in," I say. "We seem to have the same parking space."

"No, it's mine," replies Angry Parking Space Woman.

"Well, Elaine said—"

"But I'm sure Elaine gave it to you because you're probably paying more rent than I am and she's no good you know all she cares about is money so you get the space she wants me to move out I just know it because I've lived here for so long and my rent is really low because of rent control and I'm not moving no sir because I can't afford to pay the kind of rent you pay do you know that the girl in apartment ten is jealous of me because she wants my husband it's true she tried to come on to him the little bitch so watch out for her."

"Well, I think you should call Elaine to talk about this, because she gave us that parking space," I say. I want to get very far away and I want to do it very quickly. I back up slowly and walk off as I say, "It's nice to meet you."

As I head back upstairs, an African-American boy, about eight years old, sprints up behind me. "Hey!"

"Hey, what's up?" I say.

"Did you know my brother is on 'The Parent 'Hood'?"

"Nope, sure didn't."

"He is!"

Then he runs inside the apartment directly below ours. No more details. That's the kid way of conversation. They tell you the most important thing and run off. And then I have an Oh Shit thought. What if these kids want to be our adorable kid friends? What if they try to make us watch "The Parent 'Hood" with them? What if our bedroom is over their kid bedroom instead of over the one their stage-parents sleep in? What if our gay sex noise ruins their fragile childhoods? Later that afternoon, as Morocco Mole makes me take a break from my obsessive desire to organize the new place so he can drag me to my first movie at the famous Chinese Theater on Hollywood Boulevard, the one with the footprints in front, I ask him about it. "The entertainment industry will destroy those children before we ever get a chance," he says. "And furthermore, any kid who tries to make me watch that piece-of-shit show is a dead kid. What's for lunch?"

"Let's go back to In-N-Out," I say.

"I feel compelled to tell you that In-N-Out is owned by some very religious people," says Morocco.

"Are they the kind of religion that enjoys a good faggot?"

"That I don't know. It's unlikely."

"Then it doesn't concern me. If they *do* have a problem with cake-boys then in the spirit of forgiveness and in the spirit of deliciousness I will continue to eat their burgers and pray for them between each chew of succulent beef in my mouth. I'll will them to like me, personally, with my superior eating technique. The rest of the Marys can fend for themselves."

"Anyway," he says, doing that thing where he ignores every word that's just come out of my mouth, "I'm taking you to Pink's. You're getting two L.A. landmark initiations in one day."

Because Morocco Mole used to live here, he knows all about Pink's and the spiritual bent of the folks at In-N-Out. Then he moved away for a bit to go off to Texas. He hates Texas. But a job was offered in Dallas and he took it. That's where he met me. I turned his existence into a Paradise of Love and Occasional Externalized Homophobia and now there's one thing about Texas he'll never escape.

So we go to Pink's. Pink's is a hot-dog stand on La Brea that's been around for about sixty years or so. It is reported that Bruce Willis proposed to Demi Moore there, which is the kind of story I will come to find that people seem to like to tell 'round these parts. It has nothing to do with anything real, but to them it counts as a lecture credit in Hollywood History. We get chili-cheese dogs and Grape Crushes and sit under an autographed picture of David Lynch. He's signed it, "Go Pink's!"

"If you go to the website," says Morocco, "you can see pictures of famous people who've eaten here. Like Miss Nicole Kidman."

"I have a problem believing that Miss Nicole Kidman eats, much less eats *here.*"

"Well she signed a picture for them, so maybe she just had one chili dog to go. Maybe they held the bun."

Miss Nicole Kidman follows us to the Chinese. We're seeing *Eyes Wide Shut.* It's the first matinee screening of its first day of release and the enormous theater is packed with Stanley Kubrick Fan Club members playing hooky from work. I have this thing where I like to go to movies on weekday afternoons whenever I can, but I don't like anyone else to be there. I resent the public when they ruin my opportunity to have a private screening.

"What's going on that this place can be so big and so packed too?" I ask Morocco Mole. "It's a weekday afternoon. I mean, we're here too but we just moved to town and have no jobs yet. What's up with these other layabouts?"

"This isn't Dallas," says Morocco derisively, "where little-old-lady-school-marm-you got to go see movies on your summer vacation and have the place to yourself. Just because they're out in the middle of the day doesn't mean they don't have jobs. Unlike in Texas, creative people live here."

When Kubrick's name appears on screen the audience goes wild. But then the first shot of Pink's customer Nicole Kidman's naked ass earns the same response, so maybe the work-shirkers just came to see the orgy parts. Morocco leans in to whisper, "That's where the chili dog went."

Other stuff that happens:

1. Because Morocco Mole is obsessed with movies, he decides I need to meet him at the Egyptian Theater, the site of the very first film premiere that ever was. The Egyptian is very old and renovated and is now the home of the American Cinematheque, a non-profit that screens repertory. Morocco's there with Robert, his heterosexual former roommate. HeteRobert's a decent, wild-haired schlub who's also something of a fag stag. I think he may have more gay male friends than straight. That he loves Sondheim musicals, too, is more a testament to his cultural geekery than to latent suspicious fag-leanings on his own part, though. I've already made up a secret life for him where he secretly buys Ebony Jugs *magazine when no one's looking. He's also a writer. Lots of Morocco's friends here are writers. They all wade in the freelance pool with varying degrees of success. I write, too, but not for money. Mostly I've worked on zines and pro-bono music reviews for a gay magazine called* Instinct. *HeteRobert makes a living at his writing, mostly entertainment journalism. He interrupts his evening of watching the collected films of Charlize Theron—he's interviewing her on Monday—to go to the movies with Morocco. Earlier in the evening Morocco and HeteRobert went off to have sushi, my least favorite food. So it's my duty to drive myself to the theater. It's a fifteen-minute drive max, but by minute thirty I'm lost. I've managed to get myself turned around and driving south when I should be going north. I think. I'm also panicked, because being lost at night in a huge city is not something I think I'll get out of alive, like in that Emilio Estevez movie where he makes a wrong turn and suddenly he's in Danger Town and murderers are chasing him. Neither Morocco nor I will succumb to cell phone peer pressure, so I can't call him for directions. Instead I stop at a Mobil station and ask to be pointed towards Hollywood Boulevard. The kid behind the counter looks at me like I'm retarded, mumbles about it being "that way," and, after forty-five minutes behind the wheel, I arrive at the theater. Parking is eight dollars and my receipt says "Parking Concepts" on top. I wonder how they would feel if I gave them play money and wrote "Cash Concepts" on it?*

Inside the theater, Mickey One, *starring Warren Beatty—he's on the run from the mob, or is he?—has already started. I sit down, heave a sigh, lean in to Morocco, and whisper, "I hate this place. It's conspiring against me. I want to go home when this movie's over."*

"Well, yeah," says Morocco.

"No, I mean to Texas," I say.

"Go get a drink and calm down. You're being paranoid like Warren here."

"Fuck Warren Beatty," I say.

"Get in line."

2. Angry Parking Space Woman leaves more notes on our car, demanding we move. I call Elaine and beg her to make it stop. Then it stops. From that point on we get nothing but the evil eye from Angry Parking Space Woman. Our tires are going to be slashed very soon.

MARAUDER

YOU KNOW HOW in movies you'll see people who are supposed to be in Los Angeles and it'll start raining, like pouring, and then Peter Gabriel and Kate Bush start dueting, just at the exact moment when someone needs to go soul-searching? And when the people start their soul-searching moment they always end up looking up at the sky like that's where they misplaced the soul they're searching for? That rain is a big fake-out. Every single day here is exactly the same. Relentless, blinding Mediterranean sun. Mild breezes. Little white fluffy clouds. I get online to check my e-mail and AOL cheerfully greets me with the latest death toll from the giant heat wave that's sautéeing Texas right now. Besides, according to everything I've ever heard about James Ellroy–Land, no one actually soul-searches here anyway, so that's a fake-out too.

Still, temperate weather doesn't really make me happy. Meteorologically speaking, I'm a goth. If I could find the one Sisters of Mercy CD I own I'd use it in a gray-day hex induction ceremony and coerce a rain cloud to hover over our apartment. Failing that, I get greased up with some SPF 30 and head out over the Hollywood Hills, into the Valley, home of Valley Girls and…um…I don't actually know what else, besides the office of *Instinct,* the gay magazine I've been freelancing for. Today will be my inaugural welcome-to-L.A. face-to-face lunch meeting with Gabriel, the editor. Gabriel is tall and lean with jet-black hair and he uses lots of British slang, so deep, obsessive, and fascinated is his Anglophilia. He doesn't fuck, he "shags," he's not excited, he's "mad for it," he's Jewish but would love to have tea with a vicar from the Church of England, and he's the guy who gave me my first music-writing assignment back when I was a middle-school teacher in Texas. I had e-mailed him after reading the very first issue to complain that the magazine's music page was not worth reading and that I could do better. I was willing to work for no money and those magical words made sure he didn't care if I wrote about Britney Spears or the Boredoms. And for our lunch date today, heliophobe though I am, I agree to eat at the sidewalk tables outside the restaurant we've chosen, breathing in auto exhaust. It just seems like the Los Angeles imperative. A thing about the Valley, though: It's as sun-blistered on this side of the hill as it is in Texas, so I'm kind of already cured of that particular detail of homesickness.

Gabriel calls me "Chief," which I find sort of endearing. He also picks up the tab, which I find even more endearing. And finally, after we eat, he assigns me a short piece, 200 words, on a new fragrance called n10z. My first writing gig for an actual check. I leave our meeting with a press release that announces how this new bottled aroma was derived from "a same sex-pheromone discovered by scientists." I like to think that Johns Hopkins researchers worked feverishly into the night, allocating millions in NIH grant money to unlock the secrets of faggot smell-molecules. To have the privilege of contributing this very important paragraph to a national magazine is why I abandoned the honorable profession of teaching.

Back to unpacking boxes, setting up the TV, DVD player, and stereo, and then organizing more books and more CDs and more vinyl and more board games and more kitchen appliances while Morocco Mole goes off to job hunt. Personally, from an OCD standpoint, I can't really do that sort of stuff until everything's out of boxes. I have a list of tasks to accomplish and I won't deviate from that order. On little breaks from creating paths through the stuff, I walk the neighborhood feeling frightened. I know in my brain that I have no good reason to feel this way. I have a great apartment that I'm finally moving into, a boyfriend who loves me, new inherited friends who have to be nice to me whether they like me or not since I'm now part of a buy-one-get-one-free set and if they dig Morocco then they have to tolerate me too, and I now reside in the promised land that is to the United States what the United States is to the rest of the world. Southern California is the creamy Brian Wilson–filled golden sponge cake of the country. It's where everyone's having fun and tossing around inflatable pool toys and doing the surfin' bird all day. And I live in West Hollywood, which is the gay half-serving of the sponge cake, second only to San Francisco as the homosexual promised land of the West Coast. But something nagging inside me tells me I'm the tortoise who's just been bused to school on the rabbit side of the tracks. Evidence: I'm out walking. And doing it slowly. And by the way, "Nobody walks in L.A." is pretty much a big fat lie. That's because there's no place to park a car, which is one reason Angry Parking Space Woman is so *maniático* (a Morocco Mole word; it's Spanish and means exactly what it looks like it means) for keeping her spot under our building. Tough shit, though. It's ours.

Walking is how I notice the first examples of the Implant Slut species, part of my neighborhood's diversity-training seminar. All we had in Texas was different races. Here there are actors—every pretty football team captain and cheerleader from every small town in America. They were told dozens of times, "You're so cute you should be in movies," so they loaded up the truck. The actressy women do a lot of dog-walking in yoga pants and flip-flops. And those knit caps. It's summer but they're cold. Not so cold that they feel the need to put on warm shoes. It's just their hair that's cold. And they must be saving their voices for auditions because when I walk past and say, "Hi," or, "Good morning," they either ignore me, force a grim smile, or give me the PLEASE DON'T BEGIN RAPING ME face. I know I look like a lumbering marauder and that I outweigh them by a good 150 pounds, but dang. I'm nice as pie.

The Implant Sluts also like to P-A-R-T-A-Y. At those moments tending to their instrument takes a backseat to letting everyone else know how much of a fucking blast they're having, and they function as a sort of broken alarm clock, the kind that wakes you in the middle of the night even though you set it for 7:30. It's officially 3:00 A.M. when they start shrieking, "Whooooooo!" outside my open window. "Sloshy Ladies," I silently cry, "please die of alcohol poisoning."

I'm suddenly magical with elderly Russians too. After three weeks of stone-faced stares, my first Former Soviet approaches me in the supermarket and lays a "blahblahsome-thinginRussianblah" on me. I shrug my shoulders and say, "Sorry man, I don't speak Russian. I wish I did."

I add a sheepish Me Dunno look, the one that I hope effectively communicates, "This is all my fault for not learning the language before moving here."

"Ahh," says the stranger, our budding friendship aborted. But I'm kind of into the fact that he thinks I'm from the old country. I like to think it's because I'm shaped like a potato. So it's not only my fault for not understanding Russian, it's also my fault for not acquiring an un-fat gay body before arriving in West Hollywood. It confuses the oldies, who think they've got all the perverts clocked. The upside? It also confuses the queens. And in my new neighborhood, they crawl around like a colony of multicolored bugs.

My favorites are the Crystal Meth Queens. I understand that drug addiction is a very serious matter, but yet, not my problem at all. My problem is that I'm a crazily early riser but I can't clomp around the apartment or turn on the stereo for a 5:00 A.M. blast of Sonic Youth. Morocco Mole won't go for that. I need silent entertainments. The tweakers, therefore, are my new Farm Report. I awaken, make a cup of green tea, then pour myself some Cap'n Crunch and stand on my balcony waiting for one to steep and cool down, the other to sog up to edible status—that shit rips up your mouth— while the Crystal Meth Queens stagger down the block. The weekend is prime sighting time. They stare up at me and my Cap'n and they hope I'm holding. Why else would I be awake? I *must* have party materials for sale. I just smile and shovel cereal into my mouth and eventually they figure out that I'm not the Candyman.

Then comes the best part: They'll hook up with each other right there on the street. I've witnessed two actual sidewalk blowjobs already and that's pretty awesome. The moral: Drugged-out skanks don't care about anyone else's stinking rules.

Other stuff that happens:

1. *Celebrity sightings: Ileana Douglas and Patricia Arquette at a club called 360. We go there to see Wigstock fixture Jackie Beat perform. Morocco and I can't decide if the guy sitting near us is one of Madonna's* Truth or Dare *dancers. Then we decide not to care.*

2. *Next celebrity sighting: Crispin Glover at the supermarket, dressed in head-to-toe black, pushing a basket very quickly up and down the aisles and looking determined to make his double-coupon day-purchases count.*

3. *My first dim sum in Chinatown with Morocco's friend Marcus and fourteen of Marcus's closest personal friends. One of the women in our party played the grandmother on Margaret Cho's doomed sitcom "All-American Girl." I forget her name, but that's not why it doesn't count as a celebrity sighting. The true reason is that she was sort of with us. It wasn't a random sitcom actor encounter. The fame-watching game has rules and the first one is that if you're hanging out with them then it doesn't count. Also, she takes the last of the chicken feet before I can get to them, and taking food from me is instant disqualification. I've never eaten chicken feet before, which is why it took me just* this much *too long to muster my tongue nerves. To console myself, after the meal I buy our very first piece of Los Angeles furniture: a very large 3-D photo of a squirrel from a shop next to the dim sum place that sells pillows, lamps, and framed 3-D pictures of squirrels. They also have 3-D pictures of old people praying to loaves of bread and old-timey ships being tossed around on big waves.*

MUTILATOR

"YOU NEED TO get out of this apartment," says Morocco Mole.

"You need to shaddupayouface," is my totally clever retort.

"I'm serious," he says. "You're hiding here, I can tell."

"Not so," I say, because I know where he's going with this. "We saw those movies. We ate at Pink's. We had dim sum with an actor from a canceled TV show."

"Not we. You. We've been here for over a month and you're turning into Howard Hughes. You won't go anywhere unless I go with you."

"Not so, part two. I walk to the grocery store all the time."

"That's two blocks away. It doesn't count."

"Does so."

"Does not."

"Does so."

"Does not."

"Does."

"Not."

"Does."

"N't."

"Pbthpthp." (That's the raspberry sound you make when you're five and can't think of any other comeback. It's a communication staple in our relationship and you finally saw the definitive spelling of the word here first.)

"Pbthpthp back. You'll learn to like this place once you start seeing what the city has to offer."

∗ * ∗

The next day, after Morocco leaves for a job interview, I get in the car with a giant book of a city map called the Thomas Guide. First stop: record shops. I've been avoiding them for frugality's sake but I've decided that enjoying some new music will soothe me. For me, not buying records is like not eating. I find a friendly hip-hop place called Fat Beats where most of the customers and employees seem stoned, but there's nothing there that demands I own it. I enter the bad-attitude-pickled Vinyl Fetish and exit it soon afterwards. Then I discover my new favorite of the three, the tiny Destroy All Music. Destroy All Music is a lot like the indie record shops I used to work at back in Texas: small but excellent stock, friendly employees, and lots of seven-inch vinyl. I buy three albums—noise jazz people Borbetomagus, Guided By Voices, and a single of Christmas carols sung by a group of old ladies who live in some sort of nursing home. My mood has brightened. Then a car tries to run me down.

I'm standing at the corner of Hollywood Boulevard and Vermont, minding my own beeswax and waiting for the light and not trying to jaywalk at all, being very patient and calm so I can head to the next part of my walking tour, when a dude in a vintage Chevy van decides to try to take a left turn when it isn't his turn to take one, coming to a screeching halt and causing the guy behind him in a gigantic monster truck of an SUV to claim his right of way. He should be allowed to get out from behind Left Turn Douchebag by any means necessary, after all. SUV Monster Truck Motherfucker barrels up onto the curb doing 55 in a 35, takes out a gas station sign in the process, its sign-parts flying in all directions, and blasts past me so closely that I can feel the heat of his exhaust. His moral rightness may think it needs me to be its martyr, but I'm too spry. I jump back. Not gracefully. Not quick like a cat. Only like a terrified person who wants to live to complain another day. Other motorists waiting at the light, seeing it all go down, begin to laugh at me. This is not a Carrie at the prom hallucination. I see them laughing in their cars as they wait for the light to turn, all of them headed someplace where they'll tell their friends about the poor bitch who flailed and yelled and tripped over his own feet trying to get out of the way of the death car and about how pedestrians in this city are all asking for it by bothering to walk at all.

I cross the street.

I walk up Vermont.

I enter Amok.

I get yelled at in the first three minutes.

That is not what I wanted to happen.

Amok is a bookstore I've read about it in the cool magazines. They carry My Kind of Books, the kind about insane religious cults and crimes and drugs and freaks and autopsies. The messy-haired guy behind the counter starts hollering at me because there's an oversized trade paperback with a bent-up cover that's sitting on a shelf, a shelf I merely happen to be standing next to. It's been damaged by some thoughtless book mutilator who slinked in before me and ruined everything and now the Amok man thinks it's my doing. If he knew me at all, if I'd already lived here for a long time and was a faithful Amokoid and he knew my name and how respectful of books I am and how I would never do that to a new piece of merchandise in a store like this, then he wouldn't have yelled at me.

"Dude, I didn't even touch that book," I say, all calm. But actually I'm super torqued-up inside.

He half-apologizes gruffly, but as I browse the store (vintage gay exploitation books like *Gay Whore* and *The Different and the Damned* that have been waiting just for me to come fondle and purchase them) I still feel like he's watching me to make sure I'm not going around mucking things up and retaliating with even more book cover–killing. Inside I'm yelling at him, "I'M INNOCENT I TELL YOU!"

As I leave, I buy the fag-bashing books to show him that I'm no lookie-loo, to show him that I don't carry a grudge even when I've been falsely accused. I also get one more seven-inch single, because they sell those too for some reason (Polar Goldie Cats on the Ecstatic Peace label; in some circles that counts as name-dropping), and I decide to take my frazzled shopping nerves and go home.

I'm thinking that's all the sightseeing and shopping I can stand for one day. Then Plastica leaps out at me from around a corner. Plastica is a store where everything is synthetic. And as I enter through the door, which is sadly made of wood and not polystyrene, and as the short-haired woman running the place hums along to the Stereolab CD playing over the store speakers, I discover our next piece of Los Angeles furniture on a shelf: a vinyl pillow in the shape of a log. The vinyl has a simulated wood-grain pattern so it looks just like a real hardwood log, but then there's the surprise part where it's fake and soft so you can rest your weary head on it after you've been involved in an ugly street hassle and then an ugly bookstore hassle.

Other stuff that happens:

1. More neighbors. The three chicks who live on the other end of our twelve-unit apartment building? They used to be dudes. I'd suspected this already but didn't have a way of documenting it, short of asking them if they still had penises or not. Then I saw them all leave together wearing identical Transsexual Menace T-shirts. That's a club meeting I totally want to be invited to. The minor issue: Every time I greet them, they act like I didn't speak. I goad them with malicious comments like "hi" and "good morning" and, much like when I torment the Implant Sluts, they refuse to take the bait. In fact they glare like the menace isn't just a cute, cheeky T-shirt joke. I need to make those grumpy ladies some blueberry pancakes some Sunday morning and win them over.

2. Celebrity sighting: Bess Armstrong, the woman who played the mom on "My So-Called Life," riding in an elevator near the Virgin Megastore on Sunset. She's even wearing Mom clothes, those big jeans you pull up too high when you're a lady with hips. I loved that show, but Morocco says it's never the right thing to talk to the actors, so I'm all cool like I never knew her.

AGORAPHOBIA

MOROCCO MOLE HAS a job. This is good news. My eating schedule depends on that sort of thing. Him not finding employment was pretty much Fear Number One for me. The grotty trailer park thing again. Roald Dahl himself couldn't have imagined a slimier fate for a child. In fact, I'd sooner balloon up like a giant blueberry than repeat the *Gummo* lifestyle I experienced while stuck there. The cardboard box *is* coming for me, though, no matter how much money I make. It's just a matter of time.

His job is with a nonprofit company that does something with independent films. In what capacity he'll be working there I really don't know. Helping to make sure those terrible little shaky-camera movies about people with quirky character traits get seen, maybe. I try to make sure I never quite understand what he does for a living. That way I can imagine him at a desk making important phone calls to significant people. He starts sometime next week.

If there's one downside to his newfound employment, it's that now he's bugging me about how I'm going to pull *my* weight. "Yeah, I'm…um…getting myself settled and stuff. I'm on the case," I say.

"Get *more* on the case."

"Yes. Yes. I know."

"Open that case."

"All right!"

"Unpack that case."

"Yes! Fuck!"

But I'm kind of stuck. I wake up in the morning and I look out our window at the unnaturally blue sky and a palm tree stares back at me. People don't live where there are palm trees. They vacation there. The trees are like seven year-old girls dressed in slut clothes. It's wrong to be near them. Then I see a big rat in the tree—maybe it's a squirrel, same thing really—and I close my eyes to sleep more. I'm actually scared to go driving because I'm a directions tard and I get turned around easily. Then people honk at me and I have no choice but to know that they're right because I'm new and stupid and haven't figured out where things are yet. I deserve every honk I get. I'm going to turn into one of those housewives with agoraphobia who order in groceries and watch "The Bold and the Beautiful". Well, actually, thanks to the Fox Family Channel I'll be watching back-to-back episodes of "The Partridge Family" instead. For people always "on tour" in that bus, it seemed like they never really went anywhere, playing in the same supper club for audiences of old people week after week. But that's not a bad life.

When I was a kid, our local public library was my refuge from the squalor of the Adams Trailer Court. It was quiet. There were books. And I could do my homework there after school. Or just read magazines. Or think about how not popular I was. So I decide to check out our local branch library instead of job hunting. These places are like churches. You go there for peace. Nobody's trying to step up and battle you there. In a library you don't have to be all 400-foot-tall King Ghidorah with a triad of fire-breathing heads you must use to incinerate your enemies. Except that in the library I choose today, the one closest to our apartment, all my enemies are waiting for me inside. It's a cute enough place, housed in an old, appropriately library-ish building.

But:

There's mildew, enemy number one. It smells like it just rained and everything inside is wet-rotting. Also there are unbathed people, enemy number two. This isn't the stench of the homeless, the first ones you'd suspect and point the finger at for stinking up a place and whose reek is at least a comprehensible variety of filth. No, this is the B.O. of jerk-wad library patrons who drove up in cars, the same people who shove past you in the checkout-desk line—and it's a long line too, as there aren't enough employees to handle all the people who need assistance using the computers to trace their golden family lineage, who pester the beleaguered staff to answer questions about palmistry or where the *Chicken Soup for the Soul* books are located. I hear someone asking for help in finding information about "Odious Rex." This is the sort of thing going on in modern libraries.

Finally, and worst of all, there is loudness. That's the real enemy number one; the other two are slightly less horrible because they're not library-specific crimes. But noise in my church *is*. Now, I know that lately every single person in the United States thinks that they personally, individually, own the entire world, that all things are permitted for them, that nobody can tell them what to do and that if they want to talk out loud in the movie theater or answer their cell phone at the funeral then they sure as heck will and what are *you* going do about it, and if they decide to use the sidewalk as a spittoon and it hits your shoes then sorry but you hadn't oughta been standing there, you oughta get the hell out of the way. But who told these motherfuckers they could talk loudly, shout even, in a public library? Because it is, above all else, a hootenanny in this place. A wet T-shirt contest or battle of the bands is due to break out any minute. I came searching for calm, quiet politeness, and order, a cocoon from the ugly noisy world. I leave needing aspirin.

I'm about to pull out of the library parking lot. I'm waiting for a break in street traffic to make my move. And a man walks up and knocks on my car window. After regaining the composure I lose when he startles me with his window-banging, I yell, "I don't have any change right now!" Which is true. I don't. Then I look in my rearview mirror. The car behind me waiting to get out of the lot is empty. The driver's side door is open. The man standing at my window doing the knocking is its driver. "Oh shit, is my car on fire?" I ask, panicky, cracking my window to speak to him, but just a crack. They call them strangers because usually that's what they are. I might open it enough to give you my auto information should you bump me from behind, but I won't be rolling it all the way down or opening the door so you can jack me, Bub. I watch "Dateline." I know some things.

"What does your bumper sticker mean?" he asks.

"My what?"

"Your bumper sticker. Can you explain to me why you have that on your car?"

"What are you talking about?!" I have two stickers on my beat-up old 1993 VW Fox. One says "Bikini Kill" because, well, Bikini Kill was a great band. The other says "Reagan Was Worse," because, well, Reagan sucked it. I get that, to some people, this might be considered a mildly provocative thing to put on the bumper of a car. It got plenty of attention back in Texas, where "Impeach the President and Her Husband Too" sentiments were plastered to a majority of pick-up trucks. But I didn't expect much grief about it from anyone in California. It wasn't like it read "I Did It for Jodie" or anything.

So my initial freak-out that I am in some sort of potentially dangerous automotive situation is incorrect. *He* is the potential danger and he's breathing his weirdness cooties into my slightly-cracked window.

"You know what? I don't have time for a political discussion," and I reach for the window-rolling-up-right-NOW handle. He looks unhappy but returns to his car. I speed off.

Agoraphobia seems like a viable option, so I stop at Ralph's to stock up on canned food before boarding up the front door to our new place. The way I see it, it's my only choice because I'm too big to do what I see a kid in Ralph's doing. The store has big deep shopping carts and this little kid is sitting in one as his mom pushes it around. She keeps handing him items as he builds himself a little fort, burying himself in cans and paper towels and boxes of cereal. He's studying the back of a box of Corn Pops, not even aware that people like me might be envying him and his position in the world. In his mind, he's invisible and I really really want to be that, too.

Unable to find a shopping cart large enough to accommodate me and enough boxes of Cocoa Krispies to make a fort, I get a rotisserie chicken and some Sara Lee Chocolate-Covered Cheesecake Bites, go home, shower, put on pajamas, sit on the couch, and watch "Providence." It's about this woman who's a doctor—I call her Dr. Amy Grant because they kind of have the same unruly curly hair—and she lives in a parallel universe version of Rhode Island where it's always autumn and the sun is positioned in a never-ending "set." She cures kids of autism by giving them puppies. It's just the kind of show you need when you're tired and cranky and eating an entire box of Sara Lee Chocolate-Covered Cheesecake Bites. There's a reason it's on Friday night.

Other stuff that happens:

1. Continued neighbor initiation: Justin. Hot and straight and almost always shirtless, with that effortlessly cool bedhead, the kind that looks like he just finished banging his equally hot girlfriend and that's his Sex Hair. Even better is the fact that most of the time it is his Sex Hair. They have loud frequent fights and then they get busy with the loud making up. And you'd think that his trendy hairstyle would be the one I could finally master, since it seems to involve non-styling of the hair. But no, it's as much work as any other. If you just wake up in the morning with actual bedhead you rarely have the cool bedhead look. You just look like a spaz who didn't fix his hair. But then if you try to get it right and you rub too much hairstick gloop on your head then you look like Billy Idol. Either way you're fucked.

2. Celebrity sighting: Tori Spelling coming down the escalator at the Virgin Center on Sunset. She's sweaty, just having come from a gym they have there called Crunch. No makeup. Big skull. Big jugs. I like her instantly. She seems down for whatever.

DOOMSDAY

"HEY, I'M A freelance writer now," I tell Morocco.

"Well…yeah," he says. "You've been one for a while."

"No, like officially now," I say.

"You're already official, Dorko. You review music for a national magazine. That makes you a nationally published freelance music critic. But tell me why you're official now anyway because I can see you're dying to."

"*Glue* magazine, that style magazine that Vaginal Davis and Mink Stole both write for, wants *me*. I sent in some clips of my *Instinct* stuff because your friend Mark knows this chick Laurie who's the editor there. They went to college together or something. On moving day he told me I should hit her up for work. So I finally got around to sending her three music-writing clips and a little note saying that I barely knew Mark but that he blah blah blah and she just called me today."

"When did you send her clips? You didn't even tell me about this."

"I felt dumb about it so I didn't tell you in case I failed. I sent them like three days ago."

"Three days ago and she got back to you *today?* What are they paying?"

"Nothing. But I'm totally a connection-worker now."

"Uh…"

"I worked my *connections!*"

"Yes, you did," he says, patting my head. "You're a very good networker, dear. Now go out there and find something that'll bring home some cash because I got fuckin' Hummel figurines to buy."

The Gay and Lesbian Center has a weekly job assistance program. And since graduating from college, I haven't worked outside of a public school setting. I have no idea how real people go about finding jobs. I've never had to sully myself with dirty things like resumes and cover letters and I have no marketable skills besides teaching immigrant kids to say, "Is this going to be on the test?" So when I tell the center's volunteer guy about my work experience as an ESL teacher and how I'm sort of interested in maybe working part-time for a nonprofit immigration assistance organization, he spends the next twenty minutes telling me that I could make an assload of dough as an English as a Second Language entrepreneur who accumulates rich foreign clients with children who need tutoring. He's already got a business model worked up for me. "The Iranians in Beverly Hills! You'll make more doing that than in Chinatown or East L.A. They're poor over there!" he says, with an expression on his face that would suggest I'd just asked him to help me get a job cleaning service station restrooms. He's practically licking his lips at the idea of my endless future wealth. He's excited for me.

Meanwhile, the cover letter example book is sitting on the table, unopened, under his folded arms. If I could just reach over and slide it my way, or if he would just excuse himself and go get the drink of water he so clearly needs— he's got that little bit of frothy rabid dog spit at the corners of his mouth that all dehydrated people have when they talk too much—then I could look at it and pretend to listen to him at the same time.

"Do you have any other skills?" he asks.

I tell him that I'm a freelance writer, which is why I want something part-time so I can concentrate on building that hobby. This gets him all worked up again, which produces more excitement-mouthfroth. See, he works in the EN-TERTAINMENT INDUSTRY! which is AMAZING! but getting work in Los Angeles is difficult because it's all about NETWORKING! and people IN THIS TOWN! can be cruel and it's going to be tough for me to make sincere friends.

"Oh really?" I ask, finally wrangling the cover letter guide from under him and flipping through to the non-profit organization section. A quick Xerox of the page I need and I'm on my way.

(Have I mentioned yet here that I'm the King of Pancakes? My late father was the first King of Pancakes and I inherited the crown from him. I'm not going off on a tangent, either; I'm giving you vital backstory. Every Sunday morning my father used to make pancakes for us while singing along to country music. He could hit the low-note parts on every Johnny Cash eight-track he owned, which I always found impressive. I knew the lyrics to "Jackson" before I could read. My dad was such a fan, and Johnny Cash seemed such a part of my life, that I believed he must have been a long lost uncle who was just lazy about visiting. Anyway, I do that now for friends. I griddle up stunning pancakes and make all visitors listen to Ferlin Husky and Merle Haggard while they dine.)

That Sunday I make lemon pancakes for Sister Betty, Sister Laura, and Dim Sum Marcus, and I've chosen the Louvin Brothers to sing for us while we eat. They're asking me how

I like L.A. so far.

"I'm good," I lie. "Adjusting." This is the only thing I can say. These are friends of Morocco's, I barely know them, they've been nothing but great to us since we came here, and when someone asks you a question like that then it becomes your job to make hopeful statements and be casually enthusiastic about your new life and its prospects. No one wants to hear about what a whiner you've turned into since moving to the big, bad city, how you're overwhelmed by the blinding newness and fastness of it all and how you're surprising yourself by your capacity for moping and daily panic attacks, about how homesick you are, how you prefer the company of the TV and a front door locked from the inside, how you've seemingly turned into a magnet for minor social disasters in bookstores and parking lots and how total strangers aren't being as retardedly nice as you'd hoped or tripping over themselves to roll out a red carpet with the word "WELCOME" emblazoned on it just for you.

That's when Laura offers to pass my name along to a film website that needs movie reviewers. The pay is decent and it would seem that it's as easy as her making a phone call on my behalf. I thank her. Maybe a little too enthusiastically. I'm the shittiest connection-worker ever.

"Please," she says. "It's nothing. You just made me pancakes with lemon zest on them. Did you zest these lemons yourself?"

"Yeah."

"Really?" she says.

And then, as if caused by some weird long-term couple brain disease, Morocco and I announce in unison, "We have a zester."

Laura says, "That's the gayest thing I've ever heard in my life."

The lucky Laura aura hovers over our apartment because later that afternoon I receive a call from a private adult ESL school I e-mailed my resume to a few days earlier. They need someone to teach a discussion class and a writing class, five days a week, three hours a day, and can I start tomorrow?

"You realize, of course, that you've got nothing to complain about, right?" says Morocco later that day. "A teaching job that fits your exact needs and a writing job for the new cool magazine in town *and* possibly another one reviewing movies just fell from the sky into your lap. What are you going to do with that information? How will it find a home in the Doomsday scenario you've got mapped out for us?"

I have to think about it for a second.

"I'll make it fit."

Other stuff that happens:

1. Gays love to argue their romantic problems away on the sidewalk in front of our place. Qualitatively, these Screaming Queens are a lot like the Implant Sluts who go "whoooo!" but they say funnier shit. Last night's show included, "Go cheat on someone ELSE!" and then, "I'm never speaking to you AGAIN!" and finally, "I hate you! I hate you! I HATE YOU!" The Screaming Queens always end on the loudest syllable and, again, much like the Implant Sluts who go "whoooo!" tend to confine their outbursts to the hours between 2 A.M. and 5 A.M. They fight, they return home to nurse their oozing romance wounds while listening to Mary J. Blige, then they fall in love again and the ruckus starts anew. It's like a beautiful flower.

2. *Celebrity sighting: Charlton Heston. Technically, it's not a sighting that counts since we know where he's going to be and the fame-sighting game relies on chance. But the American Cinematheque at the Egyptian Theater screens* Soylent Green, *a movie Morocco is fond of saying is ninety minutes of waiting for Heston to scream, "Soylent Green is people!" We check it out anyway, and loony gun-toting codger Chuck Heston is there for a post-movie Q & A. When asked about the dark, fear-of-the-future quality of late 1960s/early 1970s science fiction films, loony gun-toting codger Chuck states authoritatively (and I'm paraphrasing, but this is pretty darn accurate), "Well, no one has posed that question to me before. I must say, though, that these pictures were unique.* Planet of the Apes...*well, it was the first spaceship movie, with us in space.... and these pictures really worked.... the great scripts and the great directors really inspired me to work in these films.... and* Omega Man...*just excellent films...I'm very proud."*

Morocco leans in and whispers, "Bedtime, Mr. Heston."

2

ANGER
September & October
& November & December

CHOKEHOLD

THE ONLY THING worse than having a job is looking for one, so the recent turn of events—I now review movies for a website called IFILM—has lowered my blood pressure a bit.

Then I speak to my first publicist that's not Sister Laura, our friend who also happens to be one. A publicist is a person employed by a studio or a publicity firm to make sure that a media event like a movie or the launching of a celebrity fragrance gets into everyone's ears, eyes, and noses. Or they publicize a person, which is weirder. Technically their job is to help the media participate in this daisy chain of public blow jobs. Unless you're nobody from nowhere. Then their job is to deny you access. They like this part of their job the best because it's the least amount of work and because "no" is the funnest word ever.

But I'm told to contact a publicist. I'm told to do this by several of Morocco's other freelancing friends. Get your name on the freelancer list, they say. Just call Publicist X at Studio X, they say. So I call.

Voice mail.

I leave a message, expecting it to be returned.

No response.

The next day I call again.

Voice mail.

I leave a message, expecting it to be returned.

No response.

The next day I call again.

I get an assistant and lay my rap on her. I explain that I'm a new freelancer for IFILM and is she the right person to talk to and if not then can she direct me to the right person?

"I'll take your name and number," she says.

No response from her publicist boss.

The next day I call again.

I get the same assistant. "Oh, yes, I told Publicist X about you. Is IFILM new?"

"Yes, I think so. I just moved here from Texas myself and I've only reviewed like one movie for them so far and I'm not sure exactly when they started up so—"

"Yeah, okay. I'm going to put IFILM itself on the list but not you specifically. Who knows how long you'll be around."

"Uh...thanks."

"You're welcome. Bye."

I'm not a real film critic. I'm a bottom-feeder. And I'm not being down on myself by saying that. I can talk about nose-in-the-air movies by Andrei Tarkovsky and Hou Hsiao-hsien and not embarrass myself. It's not my film knowledge that's in question. It's my place in the media pond. Real film critics aren't usually at the screenings I end up at. They get to see the movie earlier than I do. They have real reviews to write for real outlets. I have 150-word capsule reviews to churn out, so I attend last-minute events known as "all-media" screenings where half the audience has been recruited from promotional radio station ticket giveaways. I'm not complaining about that situation. I know my place. I'm cool with it. At least until I have to fight to get into one of them.

"Dave White," I say to the clipboard-holding woman. Her job is something akin to being a bouncer. A bouncer wrapped in a pink pashmina—it's the last day of August—and balancing on strappy four-inch heels.

"Wyatt?" asks Bouncer Babe. Am I that twangy?

"White. W-h-i-t-e."

"Hmmm. You're not on my list."

"I called the RSVP line."

"I don't have your name." There is a note of finality in her voice. I see her look past me to the next person in line. I am now expected to get out of the way so she can do her job. Fuck my job. I'm bounced. Good thing I'm fat and can use that as an excuse for being slow to move it along.

"Does that mean it got left off accidentally or...?"

"No, I'm the one who makes the list so you must not have called the RSVP line." Her unlined twenty-three-year-old eyes narrow to slits. If she stays in this job long enough they'll freeze that way.

"But...I did."

"You need to make sure you're on our mailing list in the first place. I don't even know if you are or not. I've never seen your name before. And then you have to call the RSVP line or you don't get in. Did you get this invitation from a third party?"

"No, I did not. I'm telling the truth. I'm on the mailing list and I called the RSVP line. I don't know what the problem is here but I'm not it. I called. I promise." I actually hold up my hand like I'm eight and making a Webelo pledge.

"Well, we're really full tonight, we have more people on the list than there are seats. So you'll have to stand off to the side here and let me check these other people in," she sighs.

I stand and wait. I wait for the people on the list to be checked. I wait for the radio ticket giveaway people to file in. The screening is scheduled to start at 7:30. I wait until 7:30 P.M. I wait until 7:35 P.M. I'll have to call my IFILM editor tomorrow and tell her that I couldn't get past the rope. That I didn't magically will my voice from my mouth to a recorded tape to the ear of the list-making gatekeeper. It occurs to me that maybe I died and I'm a ghost now and tape recorders won't pick up my sound waves anymore. Maybe my wish came true and I'm invisible like the fort-making kid in the shopping cart. Maybe I should have qualified that wish. Either way I'll have failed on my second time out. I'll be fired. I'll never work in this town again. I'll end up toothless and dreadlocked. I won't be allowed inside public spaces because of my violent body odor. Finally, I'll die in a corrugated refrigerator box on the concrete slope of the L.A. River, the one where they filmed the drag race in *Grease*. Other homeless people will cannibalize me. Morocco Mole will bring his new porn-star boyfriend to my funeral.

"If you can find a place to sit in there you can go in now," says the Pashminator.

"Thanks," I say. I sure told her.

Seven-forty P.M. I walk into the dark theater. It's starting. There's a spot in the very loud front row. I spend half the movie with my fingers in my ears.

Movie over, I walk out, tympanic membranes still convulsing, and head for the parking garage, stopping at the corner to wait for the light to change. Why look, here comes another out-of-control car. I can see it aiming itself for me. I have just enough time to think, "That dude isn't slowing down. He's coming straight for me and he's not planning to stop for the red light. What the fuck? How can this shit happen to me twice in the same motherfucking month?"

But I don't think those sentences in consecutive thought order. Instead they all get thought at once, piled on top of one another in a mangled word thought heap as my body picks flight from the available options of fight/or and heaves itself back up to the hedge bordering the curb. I scream at the air, a stunned, shuddering, wailing blob of fat. The car rockets through the light just in time to take an entire whole side chunk off another car turning into its lane. Again, I'm missed by what feels like about a foot. The car that's been sheared clean is, bizarrely, not disabled completely, so it rights itself and begins chasing the guy who just delivered the destroy and dash. It's the fucking *Cannonball Run* on Wilshire Boulevard.

I finally arrive home. Not dead yet. Morocco Mole rubs my shoulders. "Poor baby," he says.

"I want to go home." I try to inject extra despair and poignancy into my voice. Maybe he'll crack too and realize this has all been a big mistake and we'll dab each other's salty tears with our sleeves.

"If you go home who'll fix dinner? Do you want me to starve?"

"I'm fixin' to fix you a dinner of knuckle sandwich, is what."

"You and what army?"

I leap to my feet and administer the choke hold move I learned watching Haystack Calhoun with my grandfather when I was six and have waited thirty years to use on someone. "Love shouldn't hurt!" he sputters. "What would Oprah say about your behavior at this moment?"

I think she'd be fine with it.

Other stuff that happens:

1. Tons of celebrity sightings this week: First, Angelyne, the woman famous for absolutely nothing beyond having giant billboards of herself all around the city and for driving around in a cotton-candy pink car. She was driving south on Crescent Heights, spewing pink exhaust. Then some guy from Spin City. *Not the short one. He was standing in a theater lobby. Next was one of the chubbo VJ guys from MTV, the one I've heard is a gay. I forget his name. He was shopping in Banana Republic. I wanted to yell, "Waste of time, pal. Banana Republic hates fatties like us. Leave now before they gang up to humiliate you." Then there was a guy from that shitty movie* The Mummy. *It was the guy who wore the glasses who got his eyes gouged out by the Mummy, and here's why it was stupid: The movie establishes that this motherfucker can barely see without the glasses, and they never explain how it is that the Mummy steals two eyes that barely work and yet, post-eyeball theft, can clearly see all his other victims. You watch the movie and you're like, "Hey Mummy! Take his glasses too!" In real life if a mummy was going to steal your eyeballs he would probably have the ESP to know if you had 20/20 vision or if you were just going to be a waste of his undead time. Finally, I saw Russ Meyer at Musso & Frank, a very, very old restaurant full of very, very old people. Like Russ Meyer. His old-guy hair was flying here, matted there. I like to think it was that way because he was rubbing his old-guy head between the super-normous breasts of ultravixens. His Sex Hair.*

2. I have my very first celebrity dream. Here it is: I have this T-shirt in my real life that's black and has a white silhouette of a spiky

*mohawked guy's head on it. Underneath the head the shirt reads:
"I GUESS I WAS PUNK ONCE." In the dream I'm wearing
it and I'm in France at the Cannes Film Festival. And around the
corner comes Janeane Garofalo. She's wearing the same shirt. She
sees me and sighs and goes, "Dude, you have to go home and change
that shirt because I've just been photographed wearing mine. So go
now." I'm obedient to Janeane Garofalo and begin walking home.
That's when Drew Barrymore saunters toward me. She's wearing
shiny blue low-rise bell-bottom jeans and no shoes. Also she's topless and her major cans are swaying in the French wind. She says,
"I'll walk you home, Dave." And we walk back across the Atlantic
Ocean and the continental United States to West Hollywood. At our
apartment I change shirts and try to give her a shirt of her own to
wear but she's a hippy chick and free and nude and just refuses with
a giggle. Then we walk back to France.*

ELECTROCUTION

IN MY FIRST week of teaching English to adults at the private ESL school, I've lost a third of my students. They all show up for the first day, then the numbers dwindle. I miss the Japanese girls already, the ones who came the first three days of class and then disappeared. They had great outfits. I ask Ed, one of the other instructors, what it means.

"Their parents send them to America to get them out of their hair," he says. "They probably didn't get into a good university in Japan. So they come here, show up for the first week of class—maybe—just so they can tell their parents what's happening, and then they spend their nights out clubbing."

"Fine by me," I say.

"Don't enjoy it too much," he continues. "If the class size drops below eight they cancel it and then you're out of work. And they blame you for the missing students."

"But they're adults."

"Doesn't matter. It'll be your fault. You'll see."

Sure enough, I'm called into the main office after five days. The woman who manages the office speaks like she could use a refresher course in English conversation herself. I will later find out that she is, in fact, a former student.

"Students have drop your class. One called here and complain," she says, and then mentions the student's name.

"That person showed up for one class. During that class she slept."

"Why did you not wake her?"

"I assumed it was her choice to pay attention or not. She paid for the course."

"She said you teach her nothing," continues the office manager.

"How would she know that? She was asleep."

"You must keep the students interested."

"Look, I have eight years of experience in keeping twelve-year-olds interested, so I don't really think that's the problem. And while I concede that I have the responsibility to be engaging, adult students have the responsibility to attend class and stay awake while they're here. I will continue to do my job but I fail to see how I can do their learning for them. You can monitor my class if you'd like to watch me teach."

"If more students leave we will cancel class," she says. Our meeting is over.

The best part of this scoldy conversation is the part where I don't give a shit. I have problems of my own. If a perfectly intelligent nineteen-year-old can't get her thing together enough to make a 9:00 A.M. English conversation class that any monkey could pass if only that monkey rode her little monkey tricycle to school and stayed awake, then it's no skin off my ass.

The students who remain are the friendly, studious, dull type, definitely not the Shibuya fashion set that doesn't have time to come to school. The most notorious are a French couple, neither of them older than about twenty-one, named Frederique and Guillaume. Frederique and Guillaume are, how you say, amorous. They like to make out. They make out in the parking lot. They make out in the hall before class. They make out when I turn my back to write something on the board. When I'm facing them they hold hands. When one of them masters a verb tense or pronounces something especially well or without a noticeable French accent, they celebrate with a quick peck. Pepé Le Pew would blush at their antics. Meanwhile a clique consisting of three middle-aged Korean housewives who sit together across the room from Frederique and Guillaume are scandalized almost daily. We've all seen tongue.

I leave school Friday afternoon with no agenda. I could go home and keep alphabetizing records or books. I could go hide in a movie theater. I'm very good at that. Or I could explore the city. I could get lost and try to not panic, knowing that eventually I'll land on Santa Monica Boule-vard again and be able to navigate my way back home. So I pick the third option and head to another branch of the Los Angeles Public Library system. This one's much quieter, and they're holding a book on John Adams for Morocco Mole. That I found the one homosexual man in America whose favorite musical is *1776* is never not funny to me. And while browsing through the Dewey 700s, I find a copy of Debby Boone's 1980 autobiography, *Debby Boone So Far.* I turn to the back flap for the last check-out date: 1996. That means that only three years ago, someone in this city felt compelled to read a book ghostwritten for a one-hit Christian pop singer. I take it with me, claim Morocco's history book, and use my new library card for the first time.

Next stop, a used bookstore. I understand that Rodeo Drive or the Beverly Center or somewhere the Richies shop makes for a more L.A. moment. But I like used bookstores.

They're always about 10 percent depression. As a child I imagined that inanimate objects had feelings and that the shoes you never wore were sad about it. The same would go for books in the used bookstore down the street from my family's house. The books that never got bought gave a collective sigh every time someone walked out with a bag of Harlequin romances—they sold those by the pound—and at Christmas they wept like the misfit toys on *Rudolph the Red-Nosed Reindeer.*

Christmas. If I were home I'd be about half-finished with my Christmas shopping by this, the middle of September. It's a trait that sickens most of my friends, but I like to get it dealt with so I can spend December drinking cocoa and going to parties. The move, however, interrupted my months-long planning and purchasing momentum. I've found exactly one Christmas gift so far this year and it's here in this store—an old French-language copy of *Bonjour Tristesse,* a book from the 1950s that was the *Less Than Zero* of its day. I'll give to Morocco Mole—and beyond that I'm not feeling it. I won't know enough people by December to fill a calendar month full of party invitations anyway. I plan to have plenty of sullen alone time. Furthermore, I don't know where anything in this sprawling nightmare city is yet, money is scant, and I'm far from the home I know. I live in a twenty-four-hour country ballad.

But.

I'm here with a man who never felt at home in Texas, so now it's simply my turn. The other night, we're driving home from a movie screening on the Sony lot, where we got lost in the maze of offices and soundstages and had to have someone from the crew of Donny and Marie's pointless new talk show point us in the right direction, and there comes a moment as we roll up La Cienega in the direction of West Hollywood when Morocco exhales and, unsolicited, proclaims his unreserved love for L.A. He's inspired by the sort of Cinemascopey view of the lights from the Hollywood Hills up ahead in the distance. And it's not like he's one of those people who's just given to making pronouncements about geography. But he pronounces it anyway. Clearly there are people like him who are genuinely excited by the possibilities of Los Angeles. But really, fuck those people. This place sucks. I want my not-interesting, easy to navigate, small-circle life back.

Okay, maybe it's me who sucks.

Used bookstore eating my dust, I make my way back to the apartment and stop at my neighborhood Wild Oats grocery store for dinner-making whatevers. I may suck, but I'm determined to buck up and make my man a decent Friday night dinner of bowel-sweeping healthiness. I load up a big basket of perishables and head to the checkout line. The guy standing behind me is holding a package of batteries, so I decide he should go ahead of me. This is not a huge deal, doing this. You are not so important that you have to get back to the Batcave *now* and pick up the red phone in time to thwart the Penguin. You can wait. Waiting gives you time to think about your life and read tabloids about celebrities with cellulite who dared to go outside and show it off, or to pick up some gum or a Dark Chocolate Milky Way, except this is the healthy store and they have only gross carob shit and that's more like chocolate punishment really, but anyway waiting is good for you. I let Battery Man cut in line. He says, "My, that is *decent* of you! Thank you so much! You're a good man!"

He's freaking me out.

Then I put all my stuff on the counter, which has no conveyor belt because who knows why, there just isn't one. They're a corporate tool of the Man, I suppose. You just have to push all your items forward on the counter. I do this and the woman behind me does the same. The cashier looks at me and says, "You know what? I'm giving you the NPR-listener discount today because you're so nice. You let that man go ahead of you and you pushed all your items forward so she could put her things down too. You deserve it."

As if it couldn't get weirder, the woman behind me goes, "Oh, it's true! You *are* nice! You're not from here, are you?"

One time, Morocco and I were accosted on the street by a hidden camera show that tried to trick people into do-ing weird stunts like walking barefoot through a kiddie-pool filled with bright red house paint. We declined at the time, but I'm wondering if that show hasn't tracked me down again.

"No," I say. "I just moved here."

"Well," concludes the cashier. "That's why. You haven't learned how to be horrible yet."

But I'm trying.

Other stuff that happens:

1. Celebrity sighting: Rip Taylor at my neighborhood mail-your-own-package store. He's having a conversation with the owner about how he was recently mugged. Who would do that to a cool old dude like him? I want to tell him I used to watch him on The Mike Douglas Show, *because, you know, everyone loves to hear "I loved you when I was a kid" from a thirty-five-year-old.*

*2. I go to the Hollywood Bowl. Somehow Morocco Mole's
friend Tom Ford ("I'm the one who knows how to button his own
shirt") has extra tickets to see Ann Miller, who is, apparently, Not
Dead Yet.*

*"If we go to the Bowl," I ask, "won't we be interrupting Eric
Stoltz and Lea Thompson on their big date?"*

This receives the I Ignore You Now look.

*"You've never been there," Morocco responds. "Hollywood land-
mark, Hollywood legend, you're going," I expect the Giant Robo
punch, too, but it never happens. Sometimes not getting the punch
just increases the anxiety.*

*We drive to the show with HeteRobert. "Why are you coming to
this?" I ask. "Shouldn't you be home being straight?"*

"I'm a big fan of geriatric wilding," he says.

*Fifteen bucks to park. And no women in our group. Only twen-
ty-three homosexuals I've never met and HeteRobert. I feel suddenly
ethnic. And underdressed. Our group is the kind of gay that irons
and tucks in, all freshly cut hair and trim little waistlines. One gay
is wearing a sweater—it's 62 degrees—and that, too, is tucked in.
Because he can.*

*We take our seats and almost immediately suffer through an
electrocution of pop-opera fear, courtesy of middle-school prodigy
Charlotte Church, a child who really needs to be home in Ireland or
wherever she's from studying in seclusion with a no-nonsense con-
vent voice teacher and being forbidden to date boys or drink Coca-
Cola for the sake of her pipes instead of flying off to America so she
can lay down "Danny Boy" at the Hollywood Bowl for a thousand
faggots. Where are her parents? We cheer for her anyway because she's
just a kid, after all, but then pipe down when the announcer finally
says, "Ladies and Gentlemen, I'd like to introduce to you a legend.
A woman who made her Broadway debut in 1948!"*

I lean in to HeteRobert's ear: "She was fifty-five then."

And then BANG, there's Ann Miller, practically doing cart-wheels and belting out "I'm Still Here" and playing to the back row and giving, giving, giving. When she's done, all the tucked-inners jump up and shout, "WHOOOOOOOO!"

This prompts the chubby married ladies in front of us to turn around and smile knowingly. ("Oh yes, we went to the Bowl last night and we sat next to the Gays. They're so funny. They love Ann Miller. It's such a waste though. They're all so handsome.")

I blame a lifetime of deadpan indie rock shows, where the unwritten law is no excessive enthusiasm, for my physical inability to jump up and "whooo."

ABUSE

AT GLAMOROUS *Glue* magazine where I've just started writing about offbeat L.A. culture—a subject I know nothing about but will fake until I do—Laurie, the editor, has taken a shine to me, calling me her "protégé" and tossing me work for a fashion website. She's full of pep talks and prescriptive style announcements in which my name is suddenly "Doll." "Russian fogy chic!" has come out of her mouth more than once. I think she's pretty awesome. I'm also happy she's tossing me work for real money because writing for *Glue* is about something other than that. It's about, say, meeting Clea DuVall for coffee. She was our cover girl last issue. We talked about Yo La Tengo and then she apologized for *The Astronaut's Wife*. Not that I asked her to take the blame for it. She just volunteered. Then she tried to tell me she liked reading Herman Hesse. Because I know for a fact that no one likes to read Herman Hesse, I asked her to defend the statement, but she wasn't having my insolence. "Hey man, I don't know!" she said.

Meanwhile, for cash I write about the new trends in ladies plus-size fashion. Ralph Lauren's plus-size line is "uncomplicated," a euphemism for boring. Over at Marina Rinaldi they're full of "fresh new textures for fall."

"Like tenty chenille housecoats?" asks Morocco Mole.

"Yes, and elastic-waisted vinyl pants with a special insulin lining."

"Look, the insulin pants were *last* season," continues Morocco. *"Fat* lot you know about plus-size trends."

"Why you gotta hate the big beautiful people?" I say.

"I don't. I married you."

Except you're not allowed to use the F-word when you write about plus-size clothes. That's rule number one. Another rule of writing about fashion is you must grin and endure the Fashion People. For a piece about trends for spring 2000 I have to call Fred Segal and talk to one of their buyers. Fred Segal is a guy. Fred Segal is also a store in my neighborhood. The kind of place you walk into and see Kate Hudson getting huggy with the young, cutetastic staff because she's been shopping there since she was a fetus. But Fred Segal is not the guy I need to talk to. I need to talk to someone who makes decisions. Naturally, three phone calls yield nothing. Completely rebuffed. So I drag my friend Maryam—another recent Texas-to–West Hollywood transplant and my former next-door neighbor in Dallas and yes, I know that sounds too weird to be true but it totally is—with me directly to the store that Friday after I finish teaching. I'm going to take matters into my own hands.

On our way there, Maryam grills me for details about my exciting fashion-writing assignment. "It's not that exciting," I say.

"Yes it is!" she squeals.

"Okay, it is."

"You're right, it's not. You should be working at a car wash."

"It's just that I'm trying to accomplish what should be a relatively easy task and I'm not getting anywhere with a story I should have turned in yesterday. Hey what do you know about the Iranians in Beverly Hills?"

"What about them?"

"Well do they exist, for starters?"

"Yes, but call them Persian."

"Why is that?"

"It's just how we like it."

"But isn't your family from Iran?"

"Yeah but to the entire stupid world Iranian equals terrorist and Persian is a beautiful carpet or a fluffy kitten."

Then she tells me that, in fact, her father is about to buy a home in Beverly Hills as an investment.

"Do you have any Persian relatives from, like, Old Persia or wherever, about to move to Beverly Hills?" I ask. "If so, tell them to give me a call."

The inside of Fred Segal is an off-kilter maze of little boutiques all under one roof, and as we stand together in one of them talking about what's next in fashion, Maryam leans in and whispers, "Rod Stewart is standing about five feet behind you."

I turn and there he is in all his bleached-out, spiky-haired, tiger-striped-blazer-with-padded-shoulders, stomach-pumped, senior-citizenly splendor. He's shopping with his—what—granddaughter? Girlfriend? They're looking at stretchy, feather-covered tops. Maybe for Rod. There's not a single part of my brain where Rod Stewart holds any fascination, though, so I turn back around and continue taking notes about batik-print pants. I'm busy. That's when a voice yells, "SIR, WE DON'T ALLOW NOTE-TAKING HERE IN THE STORE!"

The tiny woman who yells at me has chosen to do it her way, and her way is the way of the foghorn. She doesn't come up to me and ask me what I'm doing or why. She doesn't quietly inform me of store policy regarding writing things on a notepad. That would be polite and discreet, and clearly I'm some kind of chubby-camouflage fashion spy sent over across the street from Miu Miu or Costume National or Betsey Johnson. I'm dirt, busted for jotting.

"And why not?" I ask, so calmly and coolly I wish I had a tape recorder catching how unflappable I am.

"Garble garble reason blah we just meow meow don't." Tone subtext = "You're ugly too. And plus-sized."

Rod Stewart has taken notice and is staring right at our confrontation. Maryam walks away like she doesn't know me. "What if I'm making a Christmas list?" I say.

"It's September."

"I'm the early bird."

"NO NOTE-TAKING! I'LL HAVE TO ASK YOU TO LEAVE THE STORE!"

"What if I stop writing them down and only take notes in my *mind?* Do I get to stay then?"

"FINE."

She stalks off. Rod keeps looking right at me. I fix my best Voltron laser-blast stare back at him. He blinks first. I win. Fashion writing is fun now. Except for the part where all my notes are useless because I suddenly remember Fall Fashion week hasn't even happened yet and the piece I've been assigned can't be written until then. Doy.

But the yelling. So much yelling. The hippie lie of Southern California that Southern California still likes to tell about and to itself, the one where everyone's stoned and happy, eating organically, surfing at Venice Beach and letting it all hang out, man, is in truth an exuberantly shouty, testy, and rude reality. The retail managers bellowing about note-taking in a shop and the lovesick Screaming Queens who live on my block are, I've decided, simply responding to the culture of failure that Los Angeles fertilizes much too effectively. People come here to see a dream come true. Then they fail again and again. Statistically speaking, famous people are less than a speck on the human map, but they all live here, the Most Popular Kids in School, rubbing everyone else's nose in it. Meanwhile they're all getting crazy and furiously mean from being on diets that never get to end.

Other stuff that happens:

1. Morocco Mole and I are in a neighborhood video store. We're opening a membership. Two employees stand behind the counter, both male, one white, one black. An old man wearing a yarmulke walks in and immediately begins complaining loudly about how his Prince of Egypt *tape doesn't work and how dare they sell him a defective tape and how he wants a refund right now. The two employees don't speak. The white guy takes the tape and puts it in the VCR.* Prince of Egypt *begins playing on the store's big screen TV, blaring. No problem with the tape. The black guy begins to explain that sometimes it's the VCR and not the tape and how if you can clean the heads—*

"I'm not talking to you," snaps the surly senior, clearly looking to start it up. "I choose to deal with him! You're not to speak to me!"

"Oh, I can't speak? You don't like black folks talking to you?! Listen to this! Your tape is fine!"

The TV is turned up even louder to an ear-splitting volume. The subtext of the moment just became text.

"This doesn't concern you!" shouts the elder.

"I fucking work here so it does fucking concern me!"

"I don't have to listen to someone like you be disrespectful towards me. I don't have to take this abuse! Give me my video! I'll
take my business and—"

"OLD MAN! IT'S SHABBAT! WHY YOU GIVIN' ME
THE RUNDOWN?!"

That pretty much ends it. The old man storms out the door.

2. Celebrity sighting: Faye Dunaway, screaming into her cell
phone in a supermarket parking lot. I assume there was someone on
the other end of the line. This happens not thirty minutes after the
video store rundown/religious war, and Morocco and I can't believe
our luck. As long as it doesn't involve us, we love a good rhubarb.

MOTHERFUCKER

ANOTHER THING THAT sucks about West Hollywood: gays who kick your car. Like while you're driving it. Yes, really. I'm on Melrose, at night, when it happens. See, Melrose is home to lots of tacky crap and stupid restaurants, so of course it's very popular. And as I drive, seven young gays in stretchy, rubbery clothes decide to swarm into traffic, right in front of my car. I slam my brakes to avoid splatting them, which, for reasons known only to them, they find the apex of hilarity. They laugh and stroll across, very slowly now, just to confirm their pedestrian authority and total assholishness. In Texas they'd be belly up like an armadillo by this point, but instead I, Zen master, simply begin driving slowly, honking my horn and yelling, "MOVE IT, JERKOS!" The jollier ones laugh even more loudly now, but one queen actually takes offense, yells "Fuck you!" and runs up to my car and begins kicking it with his clunky Fluevogged foot. I slam on my brakes again, simultaneously cracking a window enough to bark out the clever twelve-letter bad swear that you should never, ever say to a stranger. Strangers have guns they like to fire when you use the twelve-letter bad swear on them. Well, maybe not this limp-wrister. But still.

Gays like these, I don't get them. They're everywhere here, too, usually involved in the media on some level—okay, yes, technically I am, too, but dang, *I'm different*—and they just exist in a constantly grasping state of ME! MINE! It's like they saw the movie *Swingers* a few times on cable and learned how to say, "Vegas, Baby!" but didn't realize that the characters in that movie were unpleasant people you aren't supposed to imitate. So they put on stretchy, rubbery clothes and kick cars if they feel like it, or roll up to my apartment in Range Rovers at 3:00 A.M. on a Wednesday blasting M People's "One Night in Heaven," and honking horns (no, it's not a hypothetical example) so their friends will know they've come to pick them up for whatever social engagement they have to attend at 3:00 A.M. on a Wednesday. Maybe they're picking up the Implant Sluts who go "whoooo!" Maybe they're all friends.

My fashionably attired new pal Andy, an African-American gay who's no stranger to the stretchy and rubbery clothes himself, whom I've become friendly with from seeing him at all the same movie screenings, and who has recently, by his own admission, become all spiritual in a way he's tried to explain to me but that makes very little sense—something to do with expecting success and good fortune by giving your attitude a nonstop hand job—says, "You get too worked up. If they knew better they'd do better."

"Uh...what T-shirt is that from, Nomi?"

"It's *not* from a T-shirt. It's from a book I've been reading."

"Uh-huh."

"Basically, you send out negative energy and attract the car-kickers to you."

"Is that so."

"Yes, it is. Send out positive energy and you'll attract good people."

"Like you."

"Yes. Well, no, not as good as me."

The next day I exercise my positive energy at Launder-land on Santa Monica Boulevard. I try to, anyway. But I don't know how to positively energize while Shouting out a grease stain that Morocco Mole left on his best shirt. *If he knew better how to use a fucking napkin he'd do better,* I think to myself. Then I decide that if I feel happy I'll send out happy success energy. A couple of Twix from the 7-11 next door later, I feel happy. I may fail at attracting people who don't want to kick my car, scream at me in boutiques, or run me over, but I can attract candy in my sleep.

And it works. I attract a celebrity, right there in Laun-derland. Sara Gilbert, formerly of "Roseanne," walks in with a female friend and they begin folding sheets. I loved that show, so this is a good sign. That she ignores me completely is not the point. Successful people are in my laundromat. I'm in my laundromat. By extension, I'm more spiritual now. So spiritual, in fact, that I attract *another* person to me right then and there: a Warholian male prostitute. My Hustler has a stew-thick Eastern bloc accent, snaggleteeth, a wife-beater, muscles that aren't from the gym, and a whopper of a bulge in his pants. I can't help but notice this. Yes, I watch crotches. I'm a faggot. I was put on this earth to do a whole lot of that and I don't want to shirk my responsibility to human-ity. He catches me looking at what is most likely a wadded up pair of socks in his white jeans—it's too lumpy to be the real thing—approaches me, and says, "Hey man, what time you have?"

"Sorry, I don't wear a watch," and I actually do feel sorry. I have a soft spot for sex workers.

"You gay, man?"

"Yep."

"Me too, man. I come to West Hollywood for some fun. Everybody gay here. You like sex, man?"

"Yeah." What am I supposed to say? No?

Then comes the shakedown. "I need bus fare, man. I am from Transylvania."

"There's not a bus that goes there."

"I need bus to Pasadena, man. I need cigarettes. You got cigarette for me?"

"Sorry, I don't smoke."

"I tell you what, man. I suck your cock for pack of cigarettes."

"I just put my last quarter in the machine. Sorry." I'm apologizing left and right to this guy. I'm failing him on every level.

"You never have the Transylvanian love? Is good, man. I tell you."

I say, "I gotta check my dryer."

Then I turn and walk away. He does the same. But not before spitting on my car.

Other stuff that happens:

1. I go to Vaginal Davis's punk rock fag club Sucker. Vaginal Davis is an African-American, six-foot-plus, broad-shouldered, punk-rock, anti-drag drag queen, the deranged art-world flipside of RuPaul. I've been a fan since I first saw his old zine Fertile LaToya Jackson *back in the early nineties. The music at Sucker is noisy, my favorite type, and Vaginal Davis is a piece of living art. I have to concede that this wonderful thing is not something I'd find back in Texas.*

2. Thinking some kind of exercise might help me deal with stress.
I bring it up in a phone conversation with my mother, who thinks
anything that gets me to lose weight is a good idea and that it'll
"help take the negative edge off." I call my old college friend Beth
in Dallas, who sees it's me on her caller ID and picks up the phone
shouting, "I'm a fairy cowgirl princess! I'm a honky-tonk angel!"
for no reason. I ask her if she's ever done yoga. "No way," she says.
"Hey, but guess what else about me? I need tons of dental work.
I just found out. Fuckin' cigarettes. I smoke too much. I eat candy
all day. I'm three weeks away from looking like Steve Buscemi." I
forget why I called.

ASS

BEING PAID TO watch movies for IFILM has its privileges. For starters, you see the new movie anywhere from three days to three weeks to three months before the public gets a chance to buy a ticket. Sometimes the movie will screen in the same multiplexes where everyone else goes, sometimes in privately owned screening rooms rented by the distributor, and sometimes on studio lots. The lots are something of a disappointment because gladiator extras aren't milling about and nobody's ever leading an elephant from one soundstage to another. But the screening rooms there are the nicest ones.

Here is some screening room etiquette:

Be an Entitlement Queen in your mid-fifties. Don't dress your age. Have an entourage of four other late-middle-age gays. Bring the whole posse to an overbooked screening at a room that seats fifty. You know the invitation is limited to you and one guest but you know how to make things happen and how to talk to these people. You know that it doesn't matter what you do as long as you get exactly what you want. Pitch a hissy fit when the publicist tries to lay down the law, insult the publicist, threaten to call the publicist's immediate superior who just happens to be a close friend of yours. Finally, get into the screening, survey the assembled crowd, roll your eyes, and announce dramatically, while locking eyes with Dave White, "All the really *important* critics must be here tonight."

When Dave White says, "Is that why you're here?" pretend you're too important to listen. Lock your eyes on two rosy-cheeked college boys and move in for the kill. Engage them in a conversation about Cinema. Insult and negate their dopey collegiate opinions about everything because it's easy and you weren't as hot as they are when you were young. Make them qualify what they're saying. Make them take back every statement they make. Continue goading them. Feel satisfied.

Another thing to do in screening rooms is clip your fingernails. This isn't nasty at all. Everyone should do it in public, carrying around little clippers in their pockets attached to their car keys. Just let the loose nail trimmings fly where they may. Dave White will find this move especially enchanting, more so if he's sitting two seats away from you and being hit by the stray flying bits of your DNA. When Dave White gets up to move away from you, don't bother wondering why. Continue grooming yourself. Look your best!

Be a studio executive. Be visibly this because you're in a suit at a 10:00 A.M. screening and you're accompanied by two other identical Suits. Talk industry jive to one another before the lights go down. Ten minutes into the feature, answer your ringing cell phone and begin to have a full-volume, outside-voice conversation. When Dave White yells at you to "hey man, get the hell outta here with your stupid little chat or hang up!" make sure you yell back, "Fuck you, asshole!" before taking it outside. Pay no attention when Dave White flips you off with both hands and says, "Go back to ruining Hollywood, you cock!" back at you. You could buy and sell Dave White, who is nobody.

Naturally, my own screening room behavior is impeccable. HeteRobert can attest to this.

He takes me as his plus-one to a very early on-the-lot screening of an upcoming historical epic star vehicle. His job will be to interview the star, so he gets to see the film while it's still "in post." That's movie-making talk for "it's not done yet." The screening room is packed and there's a guy actually fiddling with sound knobs at a big mixing board in the middle of the room. About halfway through the pompous, historically stupid and bloated almost three-hour movie, I decide I want out. The longer it goes on, the more I hate the star of the film. I begin fantasizing about being HeteRobert, getting to talk to the star, and starting out the interview with, "So your new movie sucks shit. What does that feel like?" I imagine an earthquake turning the building to rubble. I haven't experienced an earthquake yet so this option is still alluring.

Finally it's over. My back end is numb. I decide to be clever and say, "My ass!" just loudly enough so that the people around me can hear. They don't know me. I'm nobody.

For this I get an actual slug of seriousness from HeteRobert. I've fucked up.

In the car he explains that early screenings like that are populated by people who worked on the movie. For all we know, the screenwriters and director were sitting behind us. The publicist was probably there too. These people are very sensitive to the shit they make, especially when everyone knows it's shit. His ability to get the interview depends on diplomatic behavior. And his usual straight-dude affability has been momentarily replaced by stern embarrassment. "You have to promise me you'll never say something like that again," he says. He's not kidding. I promise him sincerely that I'll behave in the future.

Still, though, fuck Mel Gibson.

Other stuff that happens:

1. *Celebrity sightings: Jonathan Schaech, star of* That Thing You Do!. *He's also the guy who ate his own semen in* The Doom Generation. *He's wearing a cowboy hat and has a fu-stache and is pushing a shopping cart at our neighborhood supermarket. The next day I see former Sex Pistol Steve Jones in the Virgin Megastore on Sunset. He's getting fat. I like that about him.*

2. *I watch the kids who live downstairs play a variation on a game my little brother and I used to enjoy as children. We called it Hot Wheels Tag. It involved chasing each other around and lacerating each other with strips of hard plastic orange Hot Wheels track. The star of "The Parent 'Hood" and his not-famous kid friends are doing the same thing with a belt. Whoever gets tagged It has to stand still and submit to a belt whipping. They're merciless and scream with laughter while they do it. It looks like a lot of fun.*

3. *Hey, the earthquake I wanted. Good thing I'm an occasional insomniac or I'd have missed it. But at 2:45 a.m. on a Saturday it happens. I'm at the dining room table enjoying Jell-O-brand chocolate pudding in the little snack pack container, when out on the roof there arose such a clatter—kidding—when suddenly there's this low rumbling noise, not all loud like Sensurround, the volume-based gimmick Hollywood developed to get asses in seats for movies like* Earthquake, Midway, Rollercoaster, Battlestar Galactica, *and, well, no others, but still, the real thing is not so loud. The floor starts to roll, funhousey, but slower. I jump up from the table and run into the bedroom. "Hey! We're having a little earthquake!"*

Morocco barely rouses himself. "You sure you didn't imagine it?"

"NO, I DIDN'T IMAGINE IT!"

He rouses himself a little bit, looks around, then says, "Well, it's over now. That's it. It's done."

I turn on the TV in the morning for proof that I'm not crazy. Sure enough, it happened out in the desert and was a pretty big one. All we felt in West Hollywood was a little wiggliness. A Wal-Mart in Barstow suffered the tragedy of all their cheap crap flying off the shelves. And what does Wal-Mart do in the face of this suffering? Call their employees in the middle of the night and tell them to come to work and restock those shelves now. This is true. They announce it right there on KTLA.

VIRUSES

"WHAT IF I went to a yoga class?" I ask Morocco Mole.

"What if I have my eyebrows tinted and my anus bleached?" he responds.

"No, I mean what if I really started exercising?"

"You," says Morocco, "are not a yoga guy."

"What's a yoga guy?" I ask.

"A douche," he says.

"I can be douchey," I protest.

"I know you can. But can you adopt the yoga lifestyle of tranquility and calm? Can you transcend your body/mind and learn to live in the yoga moment and enjoy that shitty yoga music?"

"My musical taste is not relevant here."

"Ho ho," says Morocco, pulling a random record out of its perfectly organized alphabetical order. "May I direct your attention to this, the actual music you enjoy so much when, thank God, I'm not at home. The name of the first song on this record is 'Genital Grinder.' Then there's the love ballad called 'Swarming Vulgar Mass of Infected Virulency.'"

"I don't see your point."

"You're an angry person," says Morocco. "I just pulled this one at random. It could have been any one of the dozens of hateful noise records you own. The name of this band is Carcass. There's a rotting corpse on the cover. Okay, wait, I think I just decided that you *should* go to yoga."

I call my mom in Texas to check in. She just quit a thirty-year addiction to inhaling vatfuls of nicotine, so she's in that phase of the process where she acts like she invented not-smoking. She's exercising now too. "Oh honey, yes, go to yoga. It'll help take off some of that negative edge."

"Yes, yes, the negative edge. You've mentioned it before."

I call Dallas Beth. I can hear her exhaling her non-filtered cigarette directly into the receiver. "Oh Christ," she says. "You're going down the stony end. Next it's a frizzy perm and a cupboard full of vitamins. Hey, guess what show I'm watching?"

"Which one," I ask.

"'The Smurfs.'"

"Uh… so really. Yoga. I should do it, right?"

"Yes, it sounds Smurfy."

I have this idea that yoga will, in fact, calm me down a little. I also want to be healthier, and I want to accomplish this without joining a West Hollywood gym that bleeds circuit party music into the atmosphere, one that's populated by the kind of Gay I have no interest in knowing, much less having to pay to look at take a spinning class.

But when we—I drag Morocco along—enter the yoga studio over in the part of Los Angeles known as Silverlake, a region of the city known for its commitment to "keeping it real" and being self-consciously grittier than every other part of the city, I realize my mistake. The pukey aroma of locker room sweat fills my lungs. I can taste the funk in my mouth. That's the first problem. The second one is the thin little mats the place provides for novices like me who don't have their own yet. These things don't cushion you from the floor much at all. Also, total strangers sweat on them all day. I lie on it and count the viruses I'm going to catch.

Then there are the feet of the yoga people. Why don't people pay attention to their feet? Why don't they know about pumice? Why do they think that their gruesomely long toenails with fungus living inside them are invisible to everyone else? So invisible, in fact, that they feel comfortable wearing fucking ugly sandals all around so that even more people can witness the display of their terror-peds? Why do they then decorate their freakish hooves with nauseating toe rings? I want to yell, "Clip your nasty toenails, motherfuck-ers!" and then drag them by their hair from the back of a pickup truck to the Body Shop. It's a foot oasis there. Cal-lous-erasing scrapers and peppermint foot lotion and a bunch of other podiatric beautification products so you won't of-fend people with delicate sensibilities. When I'm named king of deciding who gets to go barefoot, this world is going to be a much different place.

I also have a problem with the actual yoga. It's hard. This is a beginner's class for people who act like they've been do-ing it for years. I don't know what downward facing dog is. I don't know how to relax my inner ears. Our instructress is very nice and very calm and yet never explains what we are doing, why we're doing it, or if there'll be a special ice cream treat when we're finished. At one point, probably noticing the agony-scowl on my face because I'm unable to keep up and do more than a third of the poses while keeping my back flat and my navel close to my spine and my breath even and deep, she comes right over to me and tells me that it's my mind, and not my body, that's resisting. Well, thanks, sister, but my mind is not what you're asking me to sling over my shoulder while doing a push-up, now is it?

City Yoga is nicer. City Yoga is walking distance from our place. City Yoga smells nicer. The feet at City Yoga are well-attended. The instructor of the beginner's class doesn't crack the whip on you because you're a 250-pound man in a room full of tiny actresses. He doesn't give you any "Hey Big Guy" bullshit. He's soft-spoken and helpful. He says awesome things like, "That's good, Dave," and, "You're doing great, Dave." He's also really hot and would never wear a toe ring. And there's a doughnut shop along the walk back home. I might go back to City Yoga.

Other stuff that happens:
1. More prostitute action. They cruise me while I wash dishes. Our second-floor kitchen window looks down on the street. It's good for watching people like the eighties hair-metal guy who lives at the end of our block, the one who sometimes walks backwards up the street in striped spandex tights and a velvet cape. I'd say he looked like a member of Stryper but metal man is usually holding a glass of wine and Stryper, being conservative Evangelical Christians, were in public disagreement with alcohol. Meanwhile, at least once a week, our kitchen window makes me the object of the hookers' capitalist gazes. It's easy to spot them. They look like dusty cars, gentle layers of grime covering their muscles. They're usually shirtless. They stare up at me in the window and grin. A dog-walking muscle-gay would not stare. He'd glance up, grimace, and take a second glance to see if I was cruise-worthy. The pros have no time for that kind of extended foreplay. They grin non-stop until you stop *looking back. They're always closing. These are off-duty guys, mostly, who just want an extra five bucks for a pack of Merits. I know this because, not a week after my missed opportunity to experience the Transylvanian Love,*

another one stops me on the sidewalk in front of our building, asks for that very amount for that very reason, and offers up his mouth skills as trade. When I refuse he becomes angry and threatens to come back and "get me."

2. *Gabriel at* Instinct *wants a fun piece about odd, plastic home items for the magazine. I go back to Plastica to browse. Then I head to Robertson in Beverly Hills to some of the home interior places and see what's happening in polymer furniture from Italy. It's in one of those stores that I eavesdrop on a very excellent* Scenes from a Marriage *cell phone call.*

Woman on Cell Phone: "You're so sensitive! So damn sensitive all the time! I answer my phone like I answer it....Well, if you don't like it then don't call me.... And another thing, if you don't like it then you probably don't think much of me, either.... Why are you being like this? You're like a girl, not a grown man.... Did I marry a man or a woman? What's with you?...Get some help."

3. *Celebrity sighting: Minnie Driver. And she's driving.*

MURDER

"DECIDE, A TONGUE piercing or a P.A.?"

I ask Morocco Mole this question. I ask it from a distance of five feet. He's on the sofa. I'm on the cool wood floor. The sofa is too hot to sit on. It's a blistering Saturday afternoon in October—something about Santa Ana winds that no one seems to be able to adequately explain to me—and it's 1,000 degrees in our not-air-conditioned apartment. There's a heat wave on. It's the hot, sweaty, miserable end of a hot, sweaty, miserable week. I did get some shade, however. It was delivered on the phone by a publicist yesterday. It is the job of a publicist to be mean, which is why she felt comfortable lobbing it my way.

To facilitate accomplishing one of my many tasks as a freelance journalist—the equivalent of being a hooker with a laptop, because if you're desperate for work you'll do anything for any amount of money, ten cents a word and five-dollar blow jobs being essentially the same thing—I call a big studio publicist for help and get not only not-helped, but hindered. When she finds out I review for a dot-com, she tells me that they're proliferating at a rate that won't allow them to put me on their screening list. She's extra bitchy about it too. I hate publicists. When I offer to send her clips and a letter from my editor, she gives me her fax number. The very next day I fax the clips and the letter. The day after that I call back. She's seen the clips and the letter, she says, and she's still denying me screening list access. No reason. It's just something she can do.

Meanwhile, I lie on the cool wood floor of my gay ghetto apartment wearing nothing but grandpa-blue boxer shorts that match the blue plastic ice tray resting on my belly, and I rub ice cubes all over my body. We're watching *American History X* on cable. We're watching it because it's too hot to move and because we want to see Ed Norton get raped in prison. Ed's method-actor beef and faux swastika tattoo makes me think of sex, naturally, but also of body modification.

What? asks Morocco, already annoyed.

"A tongue piercing or a Prince Albert. Pick one," I demand.

"For me?" he says. "Neither."

"No, no. The game is pick one."

"Your game is stupid. I'm not playing."

"A bad robber has a gun to your head. He says pick one."

"The bullet, please."

"Pick!"

"Shut up because I'm watching the movie."

"Pick!"

"I'd rather die than get either."

"So many beautiful things in life to live for and you'll only have to endure a little pain and then a loop at the end of your peen. Pick one!"

"NO!"

"Pick now!"

"NO! SHUT UP, DAVE WHITE!"

Okay, let's take stock. I've spent three months in a place I still largely detest in spite of making some cool new friends, I barely have employment, my boyfriend is telling me to shut up when I'm being delightfully cute, it's so hot that steam is rising off me and some experimental filmmaker is probably about to knock on my door and ask if he can fry an egg on my stomach for his chub remake of *A Certain Sacrifice*, and we have no food in the refrigerator. Okay, we have food, we just don't have any cooling beverages, such as Hawaiian Punch, and right now I'd like a nice Hawaiian Punch.

We put on some clothes and walk to the grocery store. It's two blocks away. Grocery stores are great for alleviating feelings of acute geographical displacement and emotional upset. They all look alike is why, so you can pretend you're anywhere you want. Feeling homesick and grumpy? Go grocery shopping. Buy Otter Pops. Stick your head in your grocer's freezer and think about how awesome it would be if you could simply lick the photo of the ice cream on the Häagen-Dazs container so you could sample the new flavor. It really *would* help you decide. And there's *another* kid in a basket surrounded by cereal boxes. Is this a trend now? Is there a whole movement of kids with anxiety disorders who feel the need to hide under mounds of food in shopping carts?

The people in the checkout line are baring a lot of damp flesh. The checkers are sweating, too, even though the store is air-conditioned. Reese Witherspoon is in line in front of us and she's buying flowers. Jim J. Bullock is in the other line. It's a two-scoops-of-celebrity moment and even *they* look hot and miserable, which confuses me. I always thought fame meant you never had to be uncomfortable or sweaty or heat-rashy or jock-itchy or any of those things. It seems like everyone in the world is pissed off. Somehow this makes me happy—suddenly inexplicably happy.

On the walk home, Morocco says, "Pick one. Rich, famous, and sweaty; or poor, cool, and dry?"

"Rich," I say, "but with a fort made of cereal boxes and a zero-gauge P.A."

"I think we should see other people," he says.

Other stuff that happens:

1. Morocco, HeteRobert, our friend Craig the actor—he was in Swoon *and played either Leopold or Loeb, I can't remember—and I are eating at Jerry's Deli. Pete Sampras walks in. HeteRobert goes quietly apeshit. He'd probably give Pete a blow job if the tennis star walked up and demanded one. Actor Craig says, "Who is it?"*

HeteRobert stages-whispers, "It's Pete Sampras!"

Actor Craig's face looks no less confused.

"He's a tennis player," I explain.

"Oh," says Actor Craig with what I believe is an eye-roll move combined with an actual non-ironic harrumph. "Sports."

2. I go to the Museum of Death, located near Frederick's of Hollywood right off Hollywood Boulevard. Morocco refuses to join me. The proprietors claim that it's the only one of its kind in the world, and I'm inclined to believe them. The staff is very polite and eager to answer questions. They have a guillotine, mortician's equipment, whole rooms devoted to murder, accidents, taxidermy, the Black Dahlia, the Manson Family, a who's who of serial killers, disturbing John Wayne Gacy clown paintings created in his prison cell, and pretty much everything a person would ever want to know about kicking buckets. There's a gift shop too. My ex-boyfriend in Texas has a birthday coming up. We're still good friends, so I buy him a coffee mug with a photo of an auto accident scene on it. The best part of the Museum of Death is, when you leave, the guide sees you off with a "Be careful! Have a nice life!"

3. *Morocco and I celebrate four years of being gay together. It's the anniversary of the moment he looked at me, after nearly a year of absolutely platonic friendship, and thought, "How can I be so blind? He is perfect!" We go to a restaurant that smothers everything in garlic.*

DIABETES

"WE'RE BEING CRUISED," I say to Morocco Mole, who never notices this sort of thing.

"No we're not," he says. Then, "Who? Where?" as he cranes his neck around.

"Wow, you're so not subtle," I say. "Your three o'clock. The Beariest Bear in Bear Town over there is licking his chops at us like we're dinner."

We're at a gay comedy club, where West Hollywood's complete and total submission to all things lame and middle-brow—but it's gay so it deserves your support—strikes again. This is something I'm discovering about my little homo ghetto. Most of the gays here have all their taste in their mouths and even that's been dulled by cigarettes, apple martinis, and "party drugs." Around the corner from our apartment is a store on Santa Monica Boulevard called Gay Mart. Morocco's pet name for it is "The Newcastle Coal Store." Mine is less clever: "Penetrate My Anus Now, Please." Everything inside Gay Mart has a rainbow flag on it. Everything. Because people in West Hollywood need rainbow flags to be identified as Fag. Very few shirts there have sleeves. There are mesh jock straps on little hangers. They carry glow-sticks. Gay Mart seems to do a brisk business. And in spite of the fact that we wouldn't shop there even if our lives depended on it, we hope it stays open, if for no other reason than that their big storefront sign says "Parking in the Rear" on it.

But back to gay comedy. We wish we weren't at this particular gay comedy club, but we are. I'm on assignment for *Instinct*, writing about funny homos, and my biggest concern at the moment is that none of them showed up tonight. It's one of those places where the homosexual comics makes jokes about lesbian mechanics and Judy Garland and leather. But I'm being paid to write an article. I have to pretend to enjoy it like HeteRobert had to pretend to like the shitty Mel Gibson movie he took me to see. Anyway, it's easy to be distracted by the Beariest Bear in Bear Town's hairy eyeball moves. He approaches me and Morocco and begins laying on the self-deprecating cuteness and the charming. So yes, he was cruising us, which is fine by me. I like being admired. And strangely, we're all talking like we're suddenly best friends. His name is Dave, too.

On the drive home Morocco says, "See, this place is great. You just made a new friend."

"I'd hardly call that guy a new friend," I say. "He was nice and interesting and all, but all he wants is a little boom-boom. Also, his name is Dave, too, and there can be only one, and that's me."

"Are you being the Highlander now or Helen Lawson?" he says.

"Huh?"

" 'There's only one star in a Helen Lawson show and that's me, baby, remember?' "

"Faggot says what?"

"It's from *Valley of the Dolls!*"

"Oh yeah. Well, I was being the Highlander."

And it turns out that Dave 2 was, in fact, cruising us.

We fit the chubby, facial-hair-having pre-reqs that makes his pants tent. He was, however, also making friends. We come to learn later that's just *how* Dave 2 makes friends, by trying to hit it first, hang out later. So when he invites us to a birthday party—not his, some other guy's—we figure it's the friendly thing to do.

There's a running joke in the book *American Psycho* about the murderer not being able to tell his professional colleagues apart. That's my problem at this birthday party. There are no women here, only men. Make that only gay men. Make that only gay *bears*. Bears, for you readers who pay no attention to the bizarre intricacies of gay microcultures within the already marginalized gay demimonde, are exactly the opposite of the kind of gay you see on "Will & Grace." They tend to be un-skinny and unshaven. But like the other gays, they, too, tend to run in packs.

"We're at the Fat Fuck Petting Zoo," I say to Morocco out of the side of my mouth. To appear to whisper would be rude.

"We're fat fucks too," he sidemouths back.

"I didn't say they ain't pretty to look at. But what kind of person makes friends exclusively with people who are just like him?"

"That would only be everyone in the world."

"Oh yeah. That."

The spread is great, though. Huge cake, lots of ice cream, a smorgasbord of diabetes waiting to happen. Someone's brought a box of Ding Dongs.

The following Monday at school, I'm asked the "how was your weekend" question by fellow instructor Ed, the Eeyore of the school who's decided he finds me fascinating.

He's a struggling screenwriter who's never sold a script. He's too bitter, too early. He's a walking stereotype in ill-fitting clothes, patchy stubble, unwashed hair, and seething resentment. I say, "My boyfriend and I went to a bear birthday party."

"Your what?"

"My boyfriend."

"You're gay?"

"I thought it was obvious."

"You don't look gay. What's a bear?"

"A gay who looks like me."

"Weird."

"Tell me about it."

From that conversation into my conversation class.

"Bonjour, Dave," says Frederique, the make-out girl, her right hand locked tightly into Guillaume's left.

"Howdy."

I've served up the wrong greeting. A five-minute discussion on salutation ensues. Charlotte, a French lesbian who may or may not know she's a lesbian yet but who finds Jodie Foster and Angelina Jolie very appealing, and whose English is the best in the class, explains, in French, "le howdy." This does nothing for the middle-aged Korean housewives, who just accept that "howdy" is slang from Texas. Etymological scrutiny is for the young.

We move on to the lesson: page 183—Celebrations, Invitations, and Holidays. After failing to adequately deal with the strangely colloquial idea of Labor Day, the subject turns to Halloween. Sylvie has been to the West Hollywood Halloween street fair/blowout before. "The gays make a party," she says.

"So many gays in West Hollywood," sighs one of the Korean wives, making a limp wrist motion. "Why all in one place?"

"I don't know," I say. My own gay arrival in West Hollywood was more the result of laziness than anything else. The first apartment we looked at was the one we chose. Its location in a gay ghetto wasn't ever discussed. We were more excited that there was a supermarket and a movie theater within walking distance. I've never lived in a neighborhood where taking out the trash might be considered flirting.

"You live in West Hollywood, yes, Dave?" asks Sylvie.

"Yes, I do."

"Are you gay?"

"Yes."

Frederique and Guillaume interrupt their canoodling. "Ha!" shouts Frederique. "I say yes! Guillaume says no. I am the winner."

So. I'm a contest now.

Other stuff that happens:

1. Celebrity sighting: Jennifer Beals at my local dry cleaner, intensely engaged with one of the tailors. First she jumps up onto the alterations stool and puts on this long red wool dress and cape-thing and tells the tailor that she wants it more snug and not so drag-the-floory. When he is done pinning her she hops off the stool and whips a lacy bra out of her bag, points to one of the underwire cups, and goes, "See this wire? It sticks out. Can you cover it with some fabric or something? Because it's jabbing me right here." As she says this she's finger-poking her own boob.

2. Some brain surgeon on our block leaves two sticks of dynamite in the bed of his pickup next to a half-full can of spare gasoline. The sun's been extra evil-hot lately and so BOOM! People come running, the fire department shows up, but the only damage was to his own back window. The very next day I see the truck owner putting boxes into the charred bed as a woman screams at him for being a lying son of a bitch. She begins hitting him and he tries to get away, shouting, "Stop, baby! Stop! Why you gotta get so crazy!"

3. The stage parents and their offspring are moving out. "The Parent 'Hood" kid tells me, "I booked a movie with Greg Kinnear."

PSYCHOTIC

"I HATE LIVE theater. I hated it when we lived in Dallas and bitches we knew would say shit like, 'Hey, I'm doing a one-man show about my coming-out experience, or playing a corpse in *Bent*, or appearing in the gay men's chorus version of *The Wizard of Oz*. I'll just leave two tickets at will-call for you and Morocco. See you Saturday night!' And I know I'll hate it in L.A. Wait, I take that back. I'm not going to hate it in L.A. because I'm not *going*. I'd rather have paper cuts on both eyeballs than sit through anything less than Olivier doing *Hamlet* and that cat is dead so fuck it."

This is me refusing to go with Morocco to a play that's opening at a little theater in West Hollywood. The people putting on this show describe it as a "campy" musical version of a 1970s disaster movie. When will gays stop building intentional camp? When will blood rain down from the skies and drown everyone responsible for making me miserable the second I walk into a community theater experience?

"We're going," says Morocco Mole. "Dave 2 invited us and some other friends of his who do digital effects for one of the studios. One's a low-level producer muckity-muck, I don't know. They all seem nice enough."

"This is our eternal damnation for being gay, already playing itself out in our real not-dead-yet lives," I say. "Hell is right now."

So I put on a nice shirt and go to the theater. And it turns out that Dave 2 barely knows any of the guys who are with us. That sort of pisses me off. A lot. Then I find out that, in fact, one of the guys in the group is someone Dave 2 is trying to fuck, and Dave accepted the offer of three extra tickets just so he could sit next to his planned conquest. Then I'm a little less pissed off, because I'm totally pro-slut.

We're to pick up the tickets at will-call. Morocco and I meet Dave 2 and his Future Fuck in front of the theater. Future Fuck's two studio buddies arrive at 7:50 and we march into the tiny front lobby of the theater, a lobby that is, in actual size, about the square footage of most breakfast nooks. Luckily for us, it's already sold out, ten minutes to curtain, our will-call freebies given away to someone else who showed up earlier, and I don't know if that's "done" or not but it just got done to us and inside I'm secretly crackling with a tiny electric hum of joy and I sneak a grin in Morocco's direction. "Oh damn," I say. "Well, you can't always get what you want," and turn to leave.

"Wait, do you know who I am?" asks Future Fuck.

I turn around because I think he's talking to me. In just a short time I've become accustomed to assuming that the most assholish remark in the room is being delivered in my direction. But not this time. Future Fuck is talking to the woman behind the ticket counter. He continues to tell her that he called ahead of time to secure these seats for his group of *VIPs* and that she's just turned away nationally published critics and three major studio producers. She fights back. He gets huffy, bitchy, and, worst of all, loud.

I want to become nothing. Public scenes are only fine with me when I'm getting to deliver a verbal smack-down to, well, bitches like Future Fuck. But right now I'm a bitch by association and I want the earth to swallow me whole. Suddenly I'm socializing with *those* gays. *I'm* the Entitlement Queen demanding access to the public event. I'm the first one whose brains are splattered against the wall when the revolution comes.

So I turn on my heels and walk out of the lobby as quickly as possible. Morocco and Dave 2 follow. "I'msorryI'msorry I'msorry!" stage-whispers Dave 2. "I had no idea!"

"Holy fucking shit," I say. "All I want is to be outta here. I feel like we just robbed a liquor store."

One beat. Maybe two. And then, "Hey, we're in!"

It's Future Fuck. He's out on the sidewalk with us, motioning for us to come back inside. "No. What did you just do in there?" I say. "What the fuck was that?"

"I just told her who we were," he says. He's smiling.

"I'm not going back in there. I can't believe you just did that."

That's when he shouts in my face, "STOP BEING SUCH A DRAMA QUEEN!"

There are moments in your life when you'll remember how you had the presence of mind to say what needed to be said to the horribly psychotic person spit-yelling at you from three inches away. These are moments you relive later, recalling how you came up with the most blistering retort imaginable, the comeback Oscar Wilde or Dorothy Parker would have delivered. Or failing that, you can detail with prison-bravado the time you actually bit off another man's tongue to teach him a lesson. Then that's how you tell the story. You had the last word. You resisted the fascist state. You exacted the People's Revenge and told the grosso pigfucker how the shit was really gonna go down. You chewed up his bitten-off tongue and you swallowed it whole and then you grinned to all other comers with blood-smeared maniac's teeth. You were not fucked with. You didn't slink back into a theater with people you suddenly hated beyond all reason just to make the screaming and the scene-making stop. You didn't go along with evil and then sit through the shittiest play of all time, one that made you wish for a nice boring one-man show about a guy who collected Barbies as a child. You didn't succumb to faggot insanity.

This is not one of those moments.

Other stuff that happens:

1. Morocco has been reinstated as a member of the Los Angeles Film Critics Association. I wasn't even aware that he'd been a part of the group before he left town for Texas—apparently he wrote for a free bar rag called Planet Homo *back in the day and LAFCA was filling its sodomite diversity quota—and I'm not sure what being a member entails, but he's back in all the same. All he has to do is a little freelance film criticizing on the side to keep himself on the roster. "Do they jump you in?" I ask. "Do you have to get one of those 'Smile Now, Cry Later?' tattoos? Because I'd be kind of into that if you did have to. Get one, that is. Just so you know.* Vato. *"*

2. I turn down the opportunity to see Sleater-Kinney because the club they're playing in has no seats. Next stop, the 4:00 P.M. senior buffet at Luby's Cafeteria.

3. The aggressively unfriendly trans-ladies continue their campaign of aggressive unfriendliness. I go to pick up the mail from the row of boxes downstairs. As I walk down, I notice one of them enter-

ing their apartment. And when I get to the mailboxes, there's a black purse sitting on top of them. Now, in our building there are at least seven female residents. I could walk from door to door, risking having to speak to Angry Parking Space Woman or interrupting Shirtless Bedheaded Justin while he administers some heterosexuality to his cock-starved girlfriend. Or I could open it and check to see whose it is. I open it and wish I hadn't when I discover that it belongs to Trans Number One. I don't even know their names yet, that's how not-communicative they are.

I knock on the door. No answer, even though I've just seen her walk in.

I knock again and hear a shuffling sound approaching. The door opens a crack and she peers out at me, startled. "You left your purse on the mailbox," I say. "Sorry, but I opened it to see whose it was and—"

But that's all I can get out of my mouth before her hand snaps out of the crack and grabs the cheap, unattractive bag from my hand, and she utters a noise that sounds like "meep" from her weird bird-like face and slams the door shut again. Next time, I'm taking all the money from it and leaving it on the mailbox.

FAGGOT

ONE THING I learned at the 100-percent-bear birthday party is that I live in the wrong part of Los Angeles. Each time I introduced myself to a different fat bearded man and each time I was asked what part of the city I'd just moved to and each time I said West Hollywood, I got the same crinkled-up face in return. That they weren't aware of my belief that all parts of Los Angeles are the wrong part was irrelevant. They were simply out to zip code bash. Next to preschool T-Ball, this is the easiest to play of all the sports. All someone has to do is spit out the words "twink" or "tweaker" or "WeHo Queen" and he automatically wins that round. It doesn't take much imagination.

The thing is, though, that as harsh and inhumane as I've found Los Angeles to be, the twinks and tweakers and queens of West Hollywood are not really part of the problem. If anything, they provide me with a level of neighborhood enjoyment I've never experienced before. The Crystal Meth Queens and their early-morning sidewalk sale hijinks are never not funny, I've already learned to sleep through a lot of the Screaming Queens' loudmouthery—some have even taken to conducting their domestic disputes in the daylight hours when I can really enjoy the frenzy—and I've identified a new-to-me species, one I like to call the Dress-All-Stupid Queens. These are gays who enjoy yellow-tinted sunglasses, those symmetrically bleached low-rise jeans with room for a penis or testicles but not both at once, Prada sandals, $200 vintage concert T-shirts from Fred Segal featuring bands like Molly Hatchet that they never really liked but that read sort of butch, and the bedhead that only Justin My Hot Straight Shirtless Downstairs Neighbor can pull off. I find myself digging the Dress-All-Stupid Queens because "no" is not in their vocabulary.

Best of all, I think I've tapped into a fairly effective fighting technique for the worst of them, the Entitlement Queens who occasionally decide to step up and battle me. I needed one to avoid ever going through the sort of trauma I sustained at the theater with Future Fuck and his outsized wickedness. He was such a creep that even Dave 2 decided not to fuck him, which is saying a lot because Dave 2, I've come to learn in the short time we've known each other, is a horny bitch. I develop my new battle plan while sitting in traffic, three blocks from our apartment, and maybe "develop" is the wrong word since it just sort of happens spontaneously, the universe giving me one-eighth of a cup of my power back in one thunderous bolt, so I can't exactly take credit for its effectiveness. But either way, it's my new thing.

I'm waiting for the light to turn green and another gay's car is parallel to mine in the lane to my right. He's a Dress-All-Stupid Queen, wearing a shiny tight shirt. We're both first at the light. On my left, and waiting to cross the street, is a big muscle-guy wearing a pair of flimsy, package-exaggerating jogging shorts and nothing else but shoes and sunglasses. He's a fairly serious beefalo and has the Oompa Loompa–orange tan to prove it. I feel the stare of Driver Gay zooming past my head and drilling holes into Beefalo's monster chest and scrotum. Just then, I take my foot off the brake. My car rolls back a couple of inches before my foot presses down again. No big deal. Or so I think.

"Heh-loooooooww. I'm trying to get a look here!" hisses Driver Gay through his open window into mine.

"What?" I say, thinking he must be talking to someone else.

"Your head's blocking my view now. I can't see through you."

"You're kidding me...." I start chuckling and smile back at him, thinking we're just going to playfully exchange a wow-isn't-that-guy's-penis-rather-large-looking comrade moment.

"No! Fucking move your fat head so I can see that hot-tie!" he says, even more nastily than the first "hellooooo," something I wouldn't have believed was even vocally possible until just now when he demonstrates his ability.

The light changes at that second. It's time to go. But what's polite in this situation? Do I say "Oops, sorry I ruined your glimpse of cock?" Or do I take offense at his bitchy, impatient "heh-loooooooww."

I decide to take offense. He is, after all, probably on his way to chew out some service employee for not Knowing Who He Is. "Eat shit, faggot," I growl back. His face screws up in indignant shock. He flips me off and speeds away.

Back at our apartment, when I tell Morocco about this, he scolds me. "You just committed a hate crime."

"Oh?"

"Yes, you yelled 'faggot' in public at someone who didn't know you were gay too. That makes you a gay-basher now. Like, officially."

"Well, you knew that about me already."

"This isn't funny."

"Look, I'm a guy with very short hair and a goatee in West Hollywood and I'm driving a new-model VW Beetle. How many signifiers did the motherfucker need? Besides, he started it."

"You could have said 'asshole' or some generic insult, but you always go right to 'faggot.' You *like* scaring other homosexuals."

"Only the ones that deserve to be scared. Besides, he drove off and it ain't like I chased him. I drove off in the other direction. He seemed decidedly un-scared of me. All I left him with was a specific request."

"And an anti-gay slur. In *public.*"

"I'm not in the wrong. He was a faggot who needed to eat some shit. I just reminded him that he needed to do it soon."

Other stuff that happens:

1. It would appear that Ryan O'Neal, or at least someone who looks a hell of a lot like Ryan O'Neal, just moved to our block. This is a mystery, if for no other reason than that Ryan O'Neal is a millionaire many times over. And judging from our block, most of the people here are barely thousandaires, so it doesn't really add up that he'd be our new neighbor. But there he is, or what appears to be a kind of late-middle-aged, paunchy, broke-down version of him, Frankenstein-walking his dog up the street. Occasionally "Ryan" lets the dog off the leash and lets it mope along beside him as he air-boxes. As he punches the nothing in front of him, is he imagining Barbra Streisand? His own kids?

2. HeteRobert, ace freelance entertainment journalist, lives close by. So occasionally he'll call and say, "I'm going to Rock-and-Roll Ralph's. Want to join me?" And though our own neighborhood su-

permarket is a two-block walk from our place, sometimes I say yes. Rock-and-Roll Ralph's is kind of a scene, and I like to gawk. It's located very near the Guitar Center, hence the name. In RnRRalph's the customers are much more likely to be wearing snakeskin pants and buying cases of ramen noodles to live on after hitting the Guitar Center to drool over gear they can't afford, equipment some lame-o from Matchbox 20 just bought three each of in different colors. The only disappointing aspect of RnRRalph's is the faces of the Rockin' Customers. None of them seem very happy and this is not much of an advertisement for the Rockin' Lifestyle. "What are you getting today?" asks HeteRobert, a man who also happens to be a Basia fan and therefore not as impressed as I am to witness a dykey chick wearing a vintage Live Skull T-shirt. I say, "Cool T-shirt" to her and she just stares me down. We're not going to bond. To her I'm just another erection in the way. Before I can answer HeteRobert's question he snatches away my list and won't give it back.

"Gimme," I say.

"No," he says. "Let's see if you can function without it."

"I can't. I need lists to organize my thoughts."

"This is Rock-and-Roll Ralph's, Dave. Listmaking isn't very rock-and-roll."

"Neither are these customers. Why are the Rockin' People so frowny? They rock. Shouldn't they feel good about that?"

"They're just sad because they're not famous yet," he explains, and I believe him. He's been a celebrity interviewer for years now and knows more about the toxic craving for fame than anyone else I know. Though why anybody in their right mind would want to be famous is something I don't exactly get. Those girls on the cover of Maxim *aren't showing off their surgeries because they like to think about how teenage boys are cumming on the pages where they're splayed wide-open and nearly naked. They just want to be house-*

hold brands, like Smuckers, which HeteRobert has just successfully comparison-shopped for me and determined is the less expensive brand of seedless raspberry preserves.

3. "Why are we in the skeevy Hollywood Boulevard McDonalds, when there's so much other great food in this city? You have no excuse," says Morocco.

"My excuse is fuckin' Big Mac and fries," I say. "In fact, make that my reason. 'Excuse' sounds like I'm on trial. And my only crime is true sweet love of Big Mac and fries."

We're next in line, when out of nowhere comes an elderly Russian woman to cut in front of us. My number-one rule of life is No Cuts, by the way, and under normal circumstances I'd tell her to step off, but something in my belly tells me this is going to be good so I hold back.

"Refill my cup with clean water," she barks at the teenage Mc-Worker behind the counter. "This brown, you see? Also I want coffee." The kid looks back at her and opens his mouth as if he wants to say that there are other people actually in line that he needs to deal with first, but it's too late. She's got him by the balls and there's no way out but through. "No, no, not that coffee…other pot there… fresh? You have fresh? I want fresh…three creams and three sugars. Now bag to put it all in…no, this one is small. Give me bigger bag." He does it all for her. Then she turns away without thanking him, presumably to continue her hunt for pesky moose and squirrel. The boy looks at me, sighs, and says, "Welcome to McDonald's, may I take your order?"

"Yeah, gimme some clean water and some fresh coffee and a bigger bag!" I say, grinning.

For that he tosses us a couple of free apple pies.

ANGST

WE CAN AFFORD to go to Dallas for Thanksgiving or we can afford to buy a sofa, but not both, which kind of sucks. We need something to sit on, but I *really* need to go home to see my family and friends. Morocco fobs it off on me. "So it's your decision. You're the one who's homesick."

"Eat shit, faggot." It's all I can think to say.

"Look, if we go to Dallas that's fine. But if you've been complaining about living here, you've been complaining about living here without proper furniture even more."

This is true. We left our destroyed, hand-me-down couch back in Texas. It wasn't worth taking with us. And since then we've been sitting on chairs I love—mid-century stuff I picked up for idiotically inexpensive prices from Texans who didn't know what they had, but that don't offer much in the way of warmth or comfort. It's with Ian Curtis–level angst that I concede to the need for a sofa over a trip home to soothe my jones for a decent chicken-fried steak with cream gravy and some loving embraces and petting from my people. This means I won't be getting to visit Texas until at least the spring and I hate flying in during that time of year. Tornado season and all.

But then again, that means we get to go shopping. "I want something I can sink into," says Morocco.

"We need something that looks right with the rest of the stuff we own," I say. "And I'll know it when I see it."

This is how the argument always goes. I accuse him, rightly so I still contend, of having little to no sense of line, texture, proportion, or color; he accuses me of being controlling and unconcerned with his physical comfort. So after several days of bickering about form versus function, we compromise on a squarely built but still cushiony couch, mossy green. And there's money left over for a new lamp. I've got a boner for this chunky Jonathan Adler lamp with a big black shade. Color: tank. That means gray in Fag.

A week later they're delivered. I spend two hours deciding where they'll live and when Morocco walks in the door from work, he takes one look, crinkles up his face, and says, "This is it?"

"Is what it?" I say, but I know what he's getting at. I just can't believe he's getting at it.

"Is this the couch and lamp?"

"Did I pick them out with Bizarro You?" I ask.

"It all just looked different in the store."

"Yeah, well, so did you."

"It's just that now it feels like we live in a psychiatrist's office from 1963."

"That's appropriate, then, because you're being fucking mental. Come sit on it and make out with me."

He sits. "Cushions…" he says, changing his tune.

"Now you can sink," I remind him.

"I don't know about that. It's not the sinkiest one we could have bought. And actually I think it's the lamp that's making me feel like I'm about to be prescribed anti-depressants."

"That lamp, I'll have you know, is the Shit. That lamp is the fucking big tits of LampLand. Bitches are going to worship that lamp and then worship me for selecting it. Just wait."

The next day Dave 2 comes by to check out the furniture. "Did you *break it in* yet?" he says, leering.

"Not until it's Scotchgarded," says Morocco.

Other stuff that happens:

1. I enter the Hollywood Hills for the very first time. The real estate there is prohibitively expensive unless you're the kind of person who shits gold coins. And even then, I'm sort of surprised that anyone wants to live there. The pretzel-twisted roads in the Hills come equipped with space for one-and-a-half cars, the signs are obscured by trees, and every single home up there is either burrowed into the side of the hill or perched on sticks that look like the sort that crumble when the earth moves or rain starts to fall. It's a rabbit warren for young Hollywood to live in so no one can find them. Getting lost is just what you do when you're there. Glue editor Laurie has summoned me to the Hills-based home of the magazine's current art director. "I've only ever gotten lost in my limited Hills experience," I tell her. "So I need very explicit directions."

Laurie gives them to me and finishes by saying, "You're going to love it. It's very Play It as It Lays *up there." It is. But I still get lost. I ask directions of a man getting out of his SUV. "Who are you looking for?" he asks.*

I give him the address.

"Yes, but do you know this person? Are they expecting you?"

"Are you her publicist? All I need is for you to point me in the right direction, man."

He waves his hand in the direction of an upcoming fork in the road and walks away.

2. I'm late for a press screening for a new French movie and have to sit in the front row. The three old women directly behind me are upset about our closeness too.

Golden Girl 1: Oh my, we are so close.

Golden Girl 2: I haven't sat this close in fifty years.

Golden Girl 3: What will this do to my eyes?

GG1: It's my neck I'm worried about. Damn this theater. You know, we were in the front row at the Mark Taper Forum the other night. They spit on you in that row.

GG2: No!

GG1: It's true. Those actors have to project and they spit right on you if you're in the first row.

GG3: I have been spat upon, myself, in the front row at the Taper.

GG1: And that play was too much. That August Wilson loves his own words too much. He should have cut it down.

GG2: But that's how the Blacks are. So wordy!

GG3: Well that's their culture! You were paying for the experience of their culture!

GG1: That's no excuse for a wordy play. You know my screenplay that I'm writing? You remember that long scene I had where the characters were talking about the Civil War and getting very political?

GG3: Yes, I remember.

GG1: Well, I had to edit it! I had to pick up the pace and yet keep the essence.

GG2: Yes, the essence. That's the most important thing.

GG3: You do have a point.

3. I'm on TV. Sort of. An episode of "Sex and the City" just aired in which all the characters go to Los Angeles for some reason. To fuck men or something, who knows why. In one scene Sarah Jessica Parker is sitting on a balcony at the Standard Hotel on Sunset Boulevard—a stone's throw from our apartment—and reading an issue

of Glue, *the one with my cover story about Clea Du Vall. FAKE PEOPLE ON TV ARE PRETENDING TO READ MY ARTICLE! This means Sarah Jessica Parker and I are friends now. From this point on all I need to do with my life is something that benefits humanity and makes me a pile of dough and I'll be set.*

4. *Tom Ford is having a birthday, a bowling party in Montrose. We look it up in the Thomas Guide and realize we're going to need some time to drive out there. Montrose is far away from West Hollywood, more than two freeways away, and their bowling alley is an intimate spot. Eight lanes. We hear they shot parts of* Teen Wolf *there. But for a place that features eight lanes, there are twenty-four lanes worth of faggots packed inside.*

"Where's Tom?" I ask, when we try to get our bowling shoes and discover they're out of our sizes already.

"I can't see him," says Morocco.

"Who are all these people?" I ask.

"Friends of Tom," says Morocco.

"No one has this many friends."

"Tom does. He's lived here a long time and he knows a whole lot of gays. And someday you'll know this many people who'll adore you and want to attend your incredible L.A. birthday parties as well."

"Stop threatening me."

GORGE

"POUR ORANGE JUICE all over it and inside it too," says Dallas Beth on the phone. "Then slice up oranges and slip them under slits you cut in the skin. Shove in some garlic and rosemary sprigs too. Then wrap that bitch in like two pounds of bacon."

"Wrap a turkey in bacon," I repeat, trying not to doubt her.

"Do you want to baste it all day or do you want to enjoy your life, Gaywad?"

It's Thanksgiving. We have guests for the day. Tom Ford comes over, as does Dave 2, Actor Craig, HeteRobert, *Glue* Laurie and her green-suede-shoe-wearing friend Toast—yes, that's her actual name, short for Toastacia, and she totally wins the contest of Who's Got the Best Name in Los Angeles. I make the turkey. I've never cooked one before so I have to call Dallas Beth. She knows food secrets, like how wrapping everything in bacon makes it better. And her trick works. The turkey comes out perfectly without one wasted baste moment.

The day begins with French toast and the Macy's parade on TV. I've sent out an e-mail demanding that anyone who dares to think about mooching French toast off me has to show up in pajamas. Actor Craig does this because for him it's like theater. Nothing is too crazy for Actor Craig. He's been in a TV movie with Diana Ross.

We drip syrup on ourselves while watching the parade. "Al Roker is so Country Bear Jamboree," says Actor Craig, pointing at the Macy's Parade co-host.

"I'd still hit it," says Dave 2. Someday he's going to be the Rue McClanahan one.

Despite never having cooked a turkey, I'm still fairly handy in a kitchen otherwise, so I also make homemade butternut squash soup, stuffing, green beans, cranberry sauce, cheese rolls, and pumpkin pie. Morocco makes mashed potatoes. Plus there are Otter Pops in the freezer left over from summer. Those get eaten while people wait for dinner. And when dinner comes we gorge.

Later Toast slices her hands to ribbons on a broken glass while voluntarily washing dishes and is unfazed by the blood. She laughs it off in that Mack Daddy Lesbian way I've always admired. "I'm Toast Knievel," she says.

We pull Mystery Date out of our collection of ancient board games and HeteRobert, the lone man in the room who isn't lusting after the game's Dud character—the "nice" guys all appear to be limp-dicks, but the Dud is covered in grease and has messy hair and looks like he'd give it to you rough—wins. Naps are taken while an A&E "Biography" about Wayne Newton plays silently on the TV. I can't figure out who young Wayne looks like.

"A drag king," offers Laurie.

"Yeah. Billy Tipton," says Toast.

When night rolls in we watch Shania Twain's Thanksgiving Special. With the exception of Tom, none of us even like Shania Twain, but somehow awkwardly lame celebrity-centric holiday specials make me feel like I'm at home no matter where I'm watching them, so no one's allowed to change the channel. Tom studies it for several moments before commenting, "You just know that when she was a little girl her mother was always telling her to close her legs and she just couldn't do it."

And guests talk adoringly about the lamp. Not the Jonathan Adler one. They coo over a ten-dollar job I bought at IKEA. Morocco thinks this is proof that I made a design mistake, but all it really proves is that my taste curve is fucking miles ahead of my guests. Even so, five months ago, when I was having mini-panic attacks every day about anything and everything, I could not have foreseen this nice day. If someone had told me that I'd be happy to be here for even a moment, especially on a day when I should be in Texas with my family, I'd have laughed bitterly or told them to fuck off. Maybe I hate Los Angeles a little less now. Maybe not. And in any case on New Year's Y2K Eve when the rioting and looting and burning begins, I'll probably be back to square one.

Other stuff that happens:

1. I catch a cold about five days before Thanksgiving, nearly ruining the tale of heartwarming awesomeness you just read. But here's how to get over one, guaranteed. First guzzle Nyquil all day and all night. Drink "Throat Coat" tea even though it tastes pretty assy. Do not read books because they make your brain work too much. You may look at magazines with pretty pictures like InStyle. *You may watch lots of TV. Here are the shows that cured me:*

Ice dancing.

"Radical Surgery," where they showed a hand transplant.

"The Atheist Show" on public access, where you can learn definitively and without a doubt that God doesn't exist because the

hosts say so. *The hosts dress like they don't believe in having mirrors either.*

Indian music videos on the Indian music video channel.

And right after the Indian music videos a Japanese cartoon—no subtitles—about a little girl who doesn't want to wear this red pair of underpants. The underpants, however, have other ideas and keep floating around her head, following her wherever she goes. Finally she breaks down and puts them on. The end.

Jan Crouch.

Times Square *on the Sundance Channel.*

Female bodybuilding competition.

2. *The new downstairs neighbors and I are going to have words soon. I want the kid actor and his family back. At least they had bedtimes. The new chicks—Implant Sluts both—do not. They have Macy Gray sing-alongs. They love Macy Gray so much they must have gone to 7-Eleven and bought her cassingle off the counter while they waited for the clerk to fetch their Newports. They play that same damn song again and again. Macy tries to say good-bye and she chokes and tries to walk away but she stumbles and these women eat it up with a big spoon, absorbing it all into their saline-exaggerated, post-collegiate bosoms so they can whip it all out at karaoke night and impress each other with their ballsy new millennium female empoweredness. The new chicks also have loud Hits of the Eighties parties where a lot of "whooooo!"-ing goes down. The cops have already broken up one. Morocco's big idea for handling this is to bang on the floor. My more effective—and fun—method is to go downstairs and knock directly on their door and use the Sleepy Face and Teacher Voice combo, firmly telling them that our walls our shaking in time to "Karma Chameleon" and "Living on a Prayer," songs that were popular when they were still learning not to wet themselves and eat*

the paste. Just yesterday they were watching Mary Poppins, *loudly, and singing along to "Supercalifragilisticexpialidocious." Between choruses, they'd "WHOOOOOO!"*

SKANK

I WATCH THE special two-hour "Providence" Thanksgiving Movie because…I don't know why, I just do.

Earlier that day, though, the day after Thanksgiving, I shop with Morocco because that's what I like to do on the day after Thanksgiving. I feel like going to Neiman Marcus. I don't tell Morocco that I want to go to Neiman's because of the so-lame-even-I'm-getting-sick-of-myself homesickness excuse. But that's totally why. Neiman Marcus is Texan. When I'm in Neiman Marcus I am in Texas. Not that we can afford anything there, but that's not the point. I don't have to buy something. I focus on the older ladies with big blown-out hair. I focus on the store's weird, recurring butterfly theme. I try to imagine the person who waltzes in and buys those giant handmade four-hundred-dollar fish-shaped soup tureens from the home furnishing department, which is where we end up, staring at dinnerware.

"Wow, look at these plates," I say to Morocco.

"What, the clear glass ones?" he asks.

"Yeah, them."

"Are those for eating?"

"They must be. Look at how incredible they are."

"They're square. And the edges are not rounded off. Feel those edges," he says. "You could cut yourself on them. Easily."

"Isn't that fucking cool, though? Don't you like the idea that dinner could hurt you?"

"No," he says. "We're not buying them."

"We need an entire set of them," I say.

"First of all, they violate your personal design rule of noth-ing-must-match-and-Dave-White's-easily-bored-eyes-must-be-delighted-by-the-fresh-and-the-new-at-all-times. You're the one who's always railing against boring people and their matching dinnerware. They also violate your anti-consumer-ist, fuck-the-Man philosophy of finding our bowls and glasses and plates at thrift stores and garage sales, a philosophy, I might add, that you developed yourself to save yourself *from* yourself because you accidentally break a bowl or glass or plate on a weekly basis. And they're twenty-five bucks a pop."

"Look, what if there's a home-invasion robbery and I'm in the kitchen eating a snack on this handsome plate? The bad robbers would think I was defenseless but I could totally fucking kill a bitch with one of these plates. One slice and it's *I Spit on Your Grave*."

"Here's an idea. No."

"I see you need time to consider these plates and their magical qualities."

"I don't need any time at all. And what about the fact that they'd be all matchy-matchy?"

"If fancy people come over to eat at our house sometime, we'll need something to feed them with. Fancy people aren't down with eating dinner off a commemorative plate from the First Baptist Church of Paris, Texas."

"What say let's eat some lunch and come back to this argument that you'll never win?" says Morocco. He knows how easily distracted I am by food.

So we head up to the top level of this really gigantic Neiman's. They have a little café/bar up there. It's very sleek. Each individual seat at the bar has its own little TV screen rising up from the part where your plate of food goes. Today there's a football game playing. Donald Sutherland is sitting about five chairs away from us and he seems really into the game. We order bowls of turkey chili and a woman sits down next to us. She lets out a sigh, and then, loudly, in what sounds like an Italian accent, announces, "Why there is no fashion on the TV? There should be fashion, Italian fashion from Milan!"

The waiter boy just looks at her. Donald Sutherland is in his own world. "I want you should change this television," she continues. "The men will want to look at beautiful girls on the runway."

I think she believes that Neiman Marcus has its own in-house television studio and that waiter boy could wave his hand over it and make it turn into the Ann Demeulemeester spring 2000 collection. "You want to look at the beautiful models, yes?" She's talking to me.

"Always. Fashion, yes. But I got no beef with the TV," I say. "I'm not here to battle."

She leaves in a huff. Waiter boy walks up to us. "I sent her my 'go away' vibes," he says.

"Me too," I say.

Another woman walks up with her little girl in tow. They sit to eat. The little girl is wearing a pair of sky-blue curvy-soled Prada shoes. They have the little red stripe on the heel that says Prada. They're the real deal. This is a child who'll be shooting up the world's most expensive heroin in about five years. We eat and leave.

Next Morocco takes me to the Century City shopping "mall" in Beverly Hills. It's this totally outdoor place that includes a 1970s futuristic-looking office plaza. I may be a fan of getting caught in a crush of smug, privileged white people in an upscale shopping environment on the busiest shopping day of the year, but I'm not really into doing it out in nature. I like malls to be climate-controlled and cocoon-like. I resist its charms until Morocco tells me that back in the early seventies when it was first built, before they opened it to the public, a good chunk of *Conquest of the Planet of the Apes* was shot here. Then I'm happy.

We wander into the first store we approach, Macy's, and the first person we encounter inside is a young female customer in her twenties at the fragrance counter, a woman who really needed a parent to spank her insolent ass or slap her face about fifteen years ago to prevent her from becoming the person we see in front of us. She's the Neiman Marcus Prada child instantly grown up. She's demanding to use the store phone. The clerk hands her the receiver and dials the number.

A pause.

Huffy Twentysomething snaps, "It's the WRONG number!" slams the receiver back into the hand of the wide-eyed clerk, and stomps away. Morocco and I stare at each other for a moment.

"Want a Cinnabon?" asks Morocco.

"Ooh, yes."

There's an old Circle Jerks song called "I Just Want Some Skank." In this song they musically assault Beverly Hills and Century City, in that order. It was always just a song to me. Now, however, I finally understand. We wander around the open-air retail experience and buy nothing because all the stores suck big dead donkey dongs. Okay, there's an Aveda and they have nice candles, but otherwise it's a snooze. We decide to see a movie at the mall's fourteen-screen multiplex and select *Anywhere but Here* because we both like Susan Sarandon and because that's where I want to be right now. Dixie Carter and Hal Holbrook are standing in line in front of us. Morocco says, "I dare you to go up to Dixie Carter and do the Roaring Lion face."

"I'll need some sort of remuneration," I say.

"No, this is a dare. You do it for honor. In fact, this is a double-dog dare."

"I'll only do it on a triple-dog dare."

The Roaring Lion face is a face that Dixie herself created on her exercise video, *Dixie Carter's Un-Workout*. We own a copy. The entire video involves Dixie gently stretching herself into baby-step beginner yoga moves and facial contortions. At one point she rolls her eyes into the back of her head, sticks her tongue out down to her chin in a way that would make Gene Simmons consider chucking it all in, and emits a low growl/moan/orgasm noise for a full thirty seconds. It's pretty intense.

"I triple-dog dare you," says Morocco.

I think about it for a few moments. If I don't do the triple-dog dare then I'm a chump. "She'll hit me if I do it. Call security and have me dragged off or some shit. I decline your triple-dog dare," I say, and Morocco begins to make quiet chicken noises, shame-clucking me for my cowardice. Then Dixie and Hal buy a ticket to something else and the moment of opportunity is flushed anyway.

Here's what happens in *Anywhere but Here*:

Natalie Portman and Susan Sarandon wear really great

clothes that their somewhat impoverished characters couldn't possibly afford.

They cry.

They shop at the very same mall housing the theater we're sitting in. Part of the movie was shot here. My head begins to spin. I'm watching them walking in and out of stores we just passed on our way to the theater. My physical space has been fictionalized and it's freaking me out. I CAN'T ESCAPE LOS ANGELES FOR EVEN NINETY FUCKING MINUTES. Susan Sarandon demands I stare into the Mirror of Life. Fucking Susan Sarandon.

Movie over, I can't get out of Beverly Hills fast enough. Not even a big scoop of skank could make me stay.

Other stuff that happens:

1. I go see Stereolab and Olivia Tremor Control alone. Stereolab more or less embodies my favorite spongy, wiggly, blooping brand of Futurism, but Morocco Mole hates live concerts as much as I hate live theater, so I stag it. From my comfy seat in the Palace Theater balcony I enjoy the show, unconcerned that I'm doing so alone. It's okay that I haven't made friends who share my musical taste yet. They will come along, I tell myself. Then my brain skips the track when I see a woman standing about twenty feet away. She's wearing a vintage Marnie-style coat that looks just like one I've seen Dallas Beth wear. This chick looks like Dallas Beth too, the twin of a friend I miss, and for a second I actually think, "Oh hey, Beth!" But I snap out of it and remember where I am, which is not Dallas, and that I don't know a single person in the room. If it weren't for the fact that Stereolab is expertly droning and blipping their way through "Puncture in the Radax Permutation," I'd be somewhat bummed.

2. Celebrity sighting: the dude who played the husband on Rhoda. *In our local supermarket. "Ooh," says Morocco, "David Groh. That's a good one."*

FAT

FRED SEGAL, AS I mentioned earlier, lives in my neighborhood. The store, not the guy. The guy himself is like Willy
Wonka. No one ever sees him. They just flock to his candy.
And his candy is fashion. I know it's not especially punk rock
to like expensive clothes but the whole secondhand thing
only works for skinny vegans. All they have in my size at St.
Vincent DePaul's Thrift Store is an endless supply of grease-
stained mechanic's uniform shirts and, really, how rockabilly
can one person stand to be? So I go to the fancy stores sometimes to admire the fashions. Too bad, then, that it's *also* not
the kind that fits thickly-set gentlemen like me. I find this
out when I go to Fred Segal to find a nice shirt I can wear
to a holiday party we've been invited to, only to learn that
in West Hollywood, the letters "XL" have no actual meaning.
They're a cock-tease and nothing more. Marc Jacobs? He lies
about his XL. Paul Smith? Him too. The sales people call it
"European" sizing, which means that fat people in Europe
are just Gay Fat and not actually fat. Gay Fat is what homosexuals who gain five pounds are. Real fat is me and the fatly
famous like Drew Carey and Kevin James, men who must
be sending their personal assistant to Fred Segal before they
open the store to pick up the two XXL shirts (meaning actual XL, you following me?) that they stock in each style.

The sales whippet asks me if I've tried a big-and-tall store.

His expression is a good one, a combination of smelling-a-bad-smell, condescension and mockery. It's the "Why do you lardos insist on coming in here and bothering us? You'd think you'd have learned not to demand cool clothes by now" face. Anyway, he's got his sales associate pals to chat and do nothing with. I decide to go smell the big-and-tall candles in another part of the shop instead.

As I'm smelling, I sense someone moving into my personal space. I look up to see a girl with long blonde hair and one of those *Newsies* caps on her head standing nineteen inches—my neck size, by the way, which is why I'm in candles right now and not shirts—away from me. It's Britney Spears. Standing ten feet away is her huge bodyguard. I look at her, look at him, and retreat as gently as I can, so as not to startle her, the whole time thinking, "Look man, she came and stood next to *me*, you dig? I don't want any trouble." Being too close to celebrities may be someone else's idea of a good time, but after five months I'm already immune to their "magic."

The problem, though, is that they're everywhere you look in this damn city. You can't avoid them. I sat behind Carol Burnett in a theater. And Ron Howard. I walked out of an elevator once and all three Hansons got in. The youngest one was bouncing off the walls like he'd just eaten Pixy Stix for breakfast. And I can't exit my front door without tripping over Christina Ricci, the celebrity I've seen most. I'm up to six individual encounters with her in coffee shops, movie theaters, record stores, and foofy clothes places like this one. That girl is stalking me, for real.

These people are so everywhere that when I should be dreaming of a white Christmas, instead I'm dreaming about

Janeane Garofalo and Drew Barrymore. Friends have already weighed in the significance of that one, my first-ever famous person dream. Morocco Mole says, "Janeane is your cranky 'I hate Los Angeles' side and Drew is your 'I want to spread love and joy' side. They're fighting for dominance. Janeane will win because inside you're all grumpy and punk rock." (And by way of digression: Janeane, if you ever read this, I just want to say that those were his words and not mine. I don't think you're cranky. I strongly believe you to be one of the Not Awful ones.)

"Drew's blue pants symbolize your desire to become more spiritual, as blue is the color of the highest spiritual self, and her breasts are your desire to feel more safe and confident in your decisions," says Recently Spiritual Andy.

"Topless Drew equals you being only 97 percent gay and wanting to play with her titties," says Our Tom Ford.

I think what the dream really means is that I was happier living in a state where the only famous people were Troy Aikman and the local news anchors.

To cheer me up, the next day Morocco Mole takes me to the lowrider exhibit at the Peterson Automotive Museum. (Where Notorious B.I.G. was murdered, by the way. See? No matter where you go in L.A., a famous person has already been there and done something cooler.) I'm thrilled to be there. I love lowriders. I want one. They're the happiest cars on earth. I want to bounce as I cruise slowly down the boulevard and listen to War and Con Funk Shun and be un-circumcised and smoke cheeba. This would be an excellent way of life.

Happy to have seen them but sad that there's no actual lowrider in my immediate future, we leave the museum to get lunch and then head over to the massively crowded and annoying Beverly Center to do a little more Christmas shopping. Shirtless Buff Santa is on duty, letting anyone sit on his lap of muscles. Because I have about sixty pounds on him, I decide to make him work for his money by sitting on his lap. "What do you want for Christmas?" he says.

"Comme des Garçons, please. With a nineteen-inch neck," I say, grinning as I crush him, and suddenly feeling lots of comfort and joy.

After an awkward Santa pause, I feel his thighs do the tighten-up like my ass is part of his leg set at Crunch, and that's when he asks if I've tried a big-and-tall store.

Other stuff that happens:

1. Our Tom Ford drops by to give us a Darth Vader ornament for our Christmas tree. We hang it at the top. We needed an angel.

2. I hear Joni Mitchell's "River" playing in at least three different stores. She wishes she had one to skate away on. So do I, but dang, whose idea is it to inflict the saddest Christmas song ever recorded into the jolly retail shopping experience? Could it be that even the people who like it here hate the fact that it's sunny and temperate and that palm trees, even ones strangled in lights, taunt them with their un-Christmassiness?

3. Celebrity sighting: Halle Berry, buying mind-sizzlingly expensive gift wrap at Soolip, a fancy paper store. I'm there to check the place out. I'd heard they had nice ribbons, and I like putting nice ribbons on gifts. But I can't afford them if I plan to sneak back to Neiman Marcus and buy those dangerous dinner plates. I have priorities.

CRIME

I TAKE A break from L.A. to spend the last weekend before Christmas in Texas. So homesick am I that I am willing to fly—an activity that horrifies me until I want to pass out from the horrification—just to get back there. But as I do the death-row shuffle through LAX, breaking out in a cold sweat, I witness a sort of Christmas miracle: Rick James being pushed past me in a wheelchair. Just the sort of thing to take your mind off your future 38,000-foot death potential.

There he rolls, a man who'd survived a lifetime of challenges: busting out of L7, the Mary Jane Girls, Eddie Murphy's singing ambitions, and a successful part-time career of sex-torturing young female crack addicts in his mansion. He is, understandably, tired after all these achievements, so I don't begrudge his free ride to the gate. And you'd think a fucked-up dude like that would be doing the nursing home head-slump, maybe even drooling and brain-numb like the two-headed cows I used to like watching at the State Fair's mutant animal sideshows. But this is not the case with Rick. He is bright-eyed and alert. That's the miracle part. And if Rick isn't afraid to fly then I can be brave, too. In that moment he becomes my role model of courage.

Morocco and I spend only about forty-eight hours in Dallas, so there's really just time to see my family and a couple of close friends. They all seem very interested in L.A.'s traffic.

"How do you drive anywhere?" asks my younger brother, a devout Christian and father of three, used to dominating any freeway he gets on in his testosterone-tanked pickup truck.

"Dave would rather stay home than risk interacting with other humans," says Morocco Mole. "He might get momentarily lost while driving to a place where he might actually have a good time. This way he gets to continue irrationally hating Los Angeles and at the same time keep entertaining people with stories of how everyone there is so evil and he's so put upon."

"I've carved out my own niche," I say.

"Is there much crime?" asks my mother. "I worry about the crime."

"We don't worry about crime since we became Crips," I say. "Our homies got our back."

"I never know what you're talking about," says my mother.

And my crime-scoffing statement jinxes us. On our first night back, two days before Christmas actually goes down, we're woken at around 1:00 A.M. by a man shouting, "Fire!" He's screaming for someone to call 9-1-1. We jump out of bed and run to the kitchen window to see what's happening. There's no fire. But there's a guy on the sidewalk shrieking. Then I remember hearing once that when you're being attacked or mugged you should yell, "Fire!" which is just what this guy is doing. People will come for a fire. They'll just ignore you if you're being murdered.

We call 9-1-1 and open our windows to tell the guy we're doing it. He's been mugged at gunpoint and he's freaking out. He's not hurt, just traumatized. There must have been police nearby because two squad cars race down our street within moments, just as the muggers, having stolen a car around the block, come barreling up our street again, stupidly revisiting their own crime scene where they've just left a hysterical victim they forgot to kill. They're booking it as fast as they can make the hot vehicle move. One of the cop cars burns rubber to chase them, a pursuit which lasts roughly the length of our city block as the muggers stupidly and immediately crash the stolen car into a parked SUV.

Morocco turns to me and says, "They weren't all bad. At least they destroyed an SUV in the process."

"We're calling Brink's to come out and set us up an alarm system," I say. "I'll be damned if I'm getting home-invasioned."

"This had better not make you afraid of going out at night now," he says. "I'm serious. You'd better take a big sip from the Rick James cup of courage to keep you from turning into an even bigger fraidy-cat than the one you are."

I know he's right. I know this is most likely an isolated incident. I know that technically I'm not allowed to add it to the pile of isolated incidents with unpleasant people and their unpleasantness. I repeat to myself, "There is no pattern here. West Hollywood and Los Angeles are just places on a map. You will settle in. This is an aberration. You will not become paralyzed by random crime." Still, though. Calling Brink's ASAP.

Christmas comes and goes with gifts and food and cocoa and Rosemary Clooney singing "Count Your Blessings" as we watch *White Christmas* in retina-scorching Technicolor on Turner Classic Movies. Y2K comes and goes with no looting, no burning and no rioting, just pushy people in the supermarket trying to act all casual about buying tons of bottled water.

And my big 2000 resolution is to get my Rick James–courage together to go out at night, brave the muggers, and see bands. I was fearless once and I won't let myself get to be middle-aged and terrified of new things. And if there's one thing Los Angeles has over Dallas it's new things, especially live music. I used to get so torqued-up when a decent band showed up to play in Dallas or Fort Worth that nothing else would matter more. So first up, Low and the Danielson Famile, a doubleheader that could only make me happier if free cake and ice cream were also being served in the club. Morocco Mole refuses to join in the indie-rock geek's night out, calling the somber Low "music for bedsit miserablist saddos like you to commit suicide by." So I take Dave 2. He's never heard either band but he's the kind of man who's tireless in his pursuit of fun. And for a gay who blasts Dannii Minogue in his car as we drive to the show, he sure knows his share of people waiting in line, the seemingly coolest being a couple named Sean and Vinny. Apparently they were at the 100 percent bear birthday party too, but Morocco and I didn't meet them that night. And they fit the profile: facial hair, non-adherence to the Typical Gay look, varying degrees of belly. We're introduced, start talking about bands we like, and I decide Los Angeles has Texas beat on one more count: There are homosexuals living here with whom I share cultural affinities. Dallas may be home-sweet-home, but most of the sodomites there bored me, except for when we were committing real acts of deliberate sodomy. I learn that Sean is some sort of TV writer guy and, as if by magic, I don't miss the opportunity to insult an MTV game show I saw once, right before he gets a chance to let me know he co-produced it. Vinny does something with video games for a living. Plays them mostly, I think. He's holding a zine in his hands that some kid on the sidewalk is walking up and down the line selling for a buck. "I used to put out my own zine," I say.

"Yeah?" says Vinny.

"Yeah, it was dumb," I say.

Once inside, Dave 2 gets his mind blown by the Danielson Famile, a band of siblings and friends who dress in old-fashioned doctors' and nurses' outfits, do little choreographed (sort of) dances, and have a lead vocalist whose voice will remind you of a squealing piglet. They sing songs about The Lord. "Are they really Christians or is this just a big act?" he asks.

"They're 100 percent," I say. "Except you don't want to choke them for it."

Low's set is characteristically glacial and moody. Unlike my beloved Morocco Mole, Dave 2 responds correctly, calling them "beautiful."

"They're all Mormon-y too," I tell him, "but again, not so's you'd be annoyed by it."

A couple of weeks later, it's the Magnetic Fields on see-bands-now agenda. No loner, I take fellow Texan-in-L.A. Maryam, who's already so adjusted to her new life here that I barely see her because she's out at different rock clubs every night stalking sleeve-tattooed guys her parents would have heart attacks over. For some reason tonight she's turned it out in a floor-length black dress. Joining me and my Mistress of the Dark is Sister Betty, one half of the family goodness-team who allowed us to stay with them during our first troubled week here. Maryam lights up a clove cigarette as we head to Spaceland, the club where the MF's are playing. "Always 1986 for you?" I ask.

"Drop dead," she retorts, her smoke choking my face.

Then she smiles. It's sweet.

At Spaceland we meet a preposterously long line and, twenty minutes later, a gay interloper who wants to cut. He has Gay Voice, is how I can tell. Little does he know that my number-one life rule, as I've mentioned before, is NO CUTS. So he sidles up to me, figuring that because this is a Magnetic Fields show, he will magnetize himself to us and pretend to be our friend.

Gay Voice Guy Pretending to Be Our Friend: "Wow, is this line for the Magnetic Fields?"

Me: "Yep."

GVGPTBOF: "You mean I'm not the only one who likes them?"

Sister Betty: "Well, until today you were, yeah. You must have let it slip somewhere."

But he really means it. It's this idea simmering in the brain of fans of non-mainstream bands, and it goes like this: *I* like this band. Nobody else does. Nobody else is ALLOWED to like them because *I* like them and I am fundamentally different from other people. I am the only one who understands the true message of the band. *Me.*

We all just stare at him. Pricked by my silent and invisible porcupine quills, he un-sidles, bums a Maryam smoke ("Clove! Awesome!"), and yammers on, "You almost never hear the Magnetic Fields on the radio unless you hear them on my radio show. I play them all the time on *my* show." He's dying for us to ask him about his show, but I know that by saying nothing he'll go away faster. I resist saying, "Dude, we get it. You like them. Now stop embarrassing yourself and fuckin' get to the back of the line. No cuts." Not that I have to. Betty is dealing him the same soul-crushing glare she used on the former tenants who wouldn't leave our apartment when they were supposed to. To his continued monologue about his impeccable taste in music, she deadpans, "Is that so…Oh really…Wow." Finally he scrams. Denied.

"Thanks, toots," I say to Betty.

"No problem. That dickhead was killing me."

"You give the death-stare better than anyone."

"Thanks. I'm working on the part where their heads explode in a gushing fountain of blood. Like you wanted on moving-in day."

I can't wait to be there for that.

Other stuff that happens:

1. Holy balls, it is Ryan O'Neal. I don't know why, but it's definitely him renting a townhouse around the corner from us. I pass him on the sidewalk as he walks his big old dog and when he says, "Good morning," it's unmistakably Howard Bannister. I walk past him and into my building. When I get up to the kitchen and look out the window, I see that Ryan has stopped to let his dog take care of business. Just then, Spandex Metal Guy with the Cape walks up, holding his morning glass of wine, and they have a little chat. I would strangle a Christmas basket of puppies to know what they're saying.

2. My other New Year's resolution is to make the lives of Los Angeles's SUV-driving population more complicated. I want them to experience all the frustration I feel when they're in the oncoming lane, and it's night and their eyeball-destroying halogens are on. I want them to know my fury when I can't see around them at all. I want them to suffer on some level, to be inconvenienced. So I cut them off when I feel it's safe to do so. I poke along when I find myself in front of them, because who can blame a guy in a VW for poking along? Everyone knows those cars have no power. So I'm even more powerless when I get in front of them. If they're upset, I'm happy. I also like to ding their doors when I'm parked next to them in the "compact car only" spaces they decide to take, the ones where they're spilling way over the allotted lines. If they won't get out of my life, then I want them to pay the Dave White Toll. Having a target makes driving more enjoyable.

3

BARGAINING
January & February & March

POISONED

USUALLY WE HAVE dinner at Eat Well, a diner at the end of our block. But, one night, in a foolish attempt to get out of the eating rut we've already dug for ourselves in a very short amount of time, we think twice about our dinner destination. I suggest Silver Spoon, a place that's half-attractive and half-un. In the Hell Yes column is the seventies interior, human-sized dessert case that's like a merry-go-round of pies, not-unpleasant Monte Cristo sandwiches, and a staggering array of C-list Hollywood old people. The place is a who's who of "Hey It's That Guy" celebrity sightings. Actors whose names you've never known and never tried to learn, the ones who played every comic-relief drunk on "Barney Miller", the guy from that 1970s Right Guard antiperspirant commercial campaign—the one who'd say, "Hi Guy!" from the other side of the bathroom mirror—and Shelley Winters. She's the holy grail of Silver Spoon celebrity sightings. I hear she hangs out there on a regular basis and while Morocco's at work, I make sure to get over there at least twice a week and eat lunch in a booth where I won't miss her if she pops in. I've seen *The Poseidon Adventure* an embarrassing number of times; I can recite most of Stella Stevens's lines and all of Ernest Borgnine's "MY LINDA!" scene. Forget what I said about being immune to famous-person charm. It's kind of important to me that she walk in with the big tote bag I've always heard she carries her two Oscars in and so far I've been denied the pleasure of a half-way decent gawk.

In the Silver Spoon's Hell No column is the sad fact that the food is, at best, unmemorable. Morocco Mole thinks this is more important than my need to see Shelley Winters spoon rice pudding into her almost-octogenarian Academy Award–winning mouth. "Don't you want me to enjoy my-self?" I ask him.

"I want to enjoy my dinner more."

"You're sabotaging my assimilation into the West Hol-lywood lifestyle," I accuse.

"And you're sabotaging your chances of enjoying dinner in my company," he says.

"Okay, let's go to Eat Well and you can have the Eat Shit Faggot special."

"Can I do that alone?"

We compromise and go to a recently opened café called Cash Cow. I get a cheeseburger.

Then I get food-poisoned. I stay up most of the night vomiting. The next morning, my IFILM editor calls to ask if I'd be interested in going to a movie press junket. "What's that?" I ask.

"You go see the movie and then the next day you go to a hotel and you interview the stars and the director. Be-cause we're online we don't get access to them one-on-one so you'll be in a group of about ten other journalists."

"That sounds weird. I'll do it. And now I have to go be sick."

Before she hangs up, my editor tells me that in West Hol-lywood there's an Ayurvedic herbs store that's walking distance from my apartment. "They'll cure you instantly," she promises.

Ayurveda is an ancient Indian form of medicine. They give you mixtures of herbs and you're healed. And though it's thousands of years old, it still sounds like something a stoner dreamed up. I always give quackery a fair shake and I have nothing but cash and nausea to lose, so I head out.

I walk in to find no Indian shopkeepers. Instead there are two old Russian ladies standing at the counter, one behind and one in front. I wait for their Russian conversation to pause, then I launch into my tale of belly trouble. The woman in front of the counter becomes terrifically excited. "My friend, you are in good place!" she cries. "You sick? They make you well! This is *magic* place! You want to have one hundred women a night? They give you herb—you HAVE them!"

I'm feeling better already. Then she shouts, "You are QUEEN!" and hugs and kisses the woman behind the counter, but for half a second I think she's still talking to me. Vomiting must make me look gay. She exits, herbally ecstatic.

The woman behind the counter asks for more details about my upset stomach. I explain the problem and she leads me to the back. "Now you see Ayurvedic doctor," she says. Finally, a real Indian. He's a little man in a blue smock, seated in what amounts to a retail clothing store changing room with a sheer curtain hanging over the entrance. He asks me questions about my age (35), weight (240), bowel movements (clockwork), and family history (white trash, drunk, smoking and prone to colitis and lymphoma). Then he leaves the changing room and returns with a Wu-Tang Clan–sized bag of herbs. "You make a tea of this combination of herbs. Also take these herbal capsules. This is maduyashit, satawari, bhrin-graj, brahmi, aragbadmajja, ashwagangha, and vasaka."

Total cost to me = $38.00.

I walk home feeling scammed. Also paranoid that if a cop were to stop me I'd have what appears to be nothing more than a bag of reefer madness in my hands. When I arrive home and make the tea and it touches my tongue, it tastes like someone scraped the gunk from the corners of a bus station men's room and made a steaming hot drink out of it. It smells like the putrefying corpse of all common sense.

And an hour later I'm cured. Thank you, India.

Other stuff that happens:

1. Celebrity sighting: Sandra Bernhard, standing behind me in the supermarket. I see her once and then look away, tingling. I can't bear to look at her twice because if I get caught and she thinks I'm being creepy then I'll never forgive myself. Next to Shelley Winters she's the only person who can make me starstruck. I don't even look in her basket for fear that she'll be buying annoying Lunchables and I'll have to stop liking her.

2. Helicopters, chasing down crimes, are my new number-one nighttime sound. I wonder what would happen if one of them stopped working and plummeted into our apartment building. I think about that sort of thing late at night.

3. Apparently the Los Angeles Film Critics give awards out at the end of the year. Then they have a big dinner and the famous people all come. Morocco Mole says, "Guess where we're going?"

"Correction. Where you're *going."*

"Oh, come on. This'll be fun. Famous people and their outfits.

You love that sort of thing."

"I love that sort of thing from my couch. I can't very well crack on these motherfuckers to their faces, now can I?"

"Please go with me."

"Take Tom Ford. He's a starfucker."

"I want to show off my husband."

"To who? Oh, that's right, all the people there who give a shit about you and me. All the no one."

"Promise me you'll give it some thought and that you'll try to be considerate of what I want here."

He's always playing that life-partner card.

JUNK

HANGING FROM APARTMENT walls of way too many gays I met back in Texas—and who knows, maybe here, too—are those hideously ugly ceramic harlequin masks, clown faces half white and half black and morbidly tasteless by more than half. It's the kind of interior accessory that makes you think to yourself, "Okay, so yeah that thing is a nasty piece of shit, but the person I just had sex with thought it was beautiful." And then you're unsettled by the way you saw that guy in a bar and thought he was hot enough to bang but that somehow you should have seen through him a little better. You got laid, but you also got a little tackiness dust on you.

That's what a movie press junket is like.

At a movie press junket you spend the day in a lush hotel suite lobbing comfy questions at actors with a movie to promote. You, the journalist, get lots of free things. You get to see a free movie. You get a free meal or two. You get free movie promo trinkets: T-shirts, CDs, baseball caps, buttons, all kinds of things that can be sold later on eBay or at a garage sale. There's nothing bad about any of that. The actors are usually on their best behavior. Except Julia Roberts, who can be curt to press people she thinks are dumb. Or so I hear.

Then there's the flipside of the junket. The part where

you have deal with other journalists. That's where the shit gets dusty.

"Michael Douglas will be arriving in a few moments," says the publicist to the dozen or so journalists seated around a large table in this hotel suite. "It's important that the questions be related to the film and not so much about his personal life. You'll have a short time with him so be considerate of your fellow journalists." I'm stunned that these guidelines are delivered in a calm, rational tone of voice and not in the manner of a scoldy third-grade teacher, because that's how publicists usually speak.

In walks Michael Douglas.

Within two minutes, questions about the movie itself are abandoned. The first person to cross over from What-Drew-You-to-This-Role Land to How-About-the-Rack-On-Your-Hot-Young-Wife Town is a woman with a slight Italian accent who seems to be roughly the same age as my mom. Practically breathless with horniness, she pants, "I think you are one of Hollywood's sexiest actors. Why, then, do you appear in this movie unshaven and wearing a woman's bathrobe? Where is *my* Michael?"

Her Michael answers her with a benign comment about stretching for the role.

The remaining twenty minutes are spent belly-flopping straight from the high board into the invasive personal question pool:

"How do you feel about the way the press has treated your relationship with Catherine Zeta-Jones?"

"When is the baby due?"

"Is it a boy or a girl?"

"Do you want a boy or a girl?"

"If it's a boy, what will you name it?"

I sit, letting my tape player soak up Douglas's gentlemanly yet deflective answers.

He's *rico suave* in the most old-school Hollywood royalty way possible, charming this group of the easily charmed and still evading all the questions. I sit and imagine questions of my own that I don't dare lob his way: "Does CZ Jones have an even younger sister, and if so will you be keeping her around as a nanny that you hump on the side?" and "Do you have a spare $10,000 to give me right now?" and "If the baby is born intersexed, will you eliminate its ambiguous penis and raise it female?"

Michael Douglas is ushered out.

The assembled press, some from radio and some from on-line outlets, are almost unanimously odd in one way or another. Comb-over guys in Cosby sweaters or sad-ass Members Only jackets they've had since 1987. Giant satchels of papers and folders and junk. The women are blousy, air-kiss delivery systems. Lots of makeup. Lots of jewelry. Same big bags of stuff by their sides.

Next up, Tobey Maguire is chaperoned into our mouth-breathing air space. He looks like he just woke up; his owl-eyes have that morning droop. He hasn't shaved. He's wearing a v-neck T-shirt he may have actually slept in. Because he's young, he's less gracious with the questions, more snarky, but he's also perfected a gentle, cuddly form of sarcasm that floats on a cloud of cuteness above all our heads.

Question: "What has fame brought you?"

Tobey Answer: "Nothing. Money, on the other hand has brought me some nice furniture."

Question: "If your character in the movie were a real person, would you go to dinner with him?"

Tobey Answer: "Oh, of course. I like him."

Question: "Where would you go? And what would you eat?"

Tobey Answer (delivered with a look that, to me, says, "What the fuck are you on and can I have some too?" but I could just be projecting): "I…I have no idea…"

Question: "Was Robert Downey, Jr., under house arrest during the making of this movie? Did he appear sober to you?" (Dang, I wish I'd thought to ask that one.)

Tobey Answer: "I don't know. I don't know how to answer a question…um…like that."

Question: "Now that you're more famous, are you able to walk around just as Tobey?"

Tobey Answer: "Whenever I walk around, it's always as Tobey."

This answer makes me laugh in a way that can only be described as a guffaw. I actually make a snorting sound before ripping off a "HAW HAW HAW." I'm too loud. Much too loud. Several other people around the table stab me with their eyes. I look at Tobey Maguire. He seems pleased with himself.

Tobey Maguire is allowed to leave the room after this question. I get a few more grumpy looks from journalists who are probably convinced that my laughter caused their short-bus questions to be cut even shorter.

I sit, still trying to suppress a laugh. The journalists compare notes. They loved Michael, but the kid? Not as much. They tend to call the celebrities by their first names, like they're talking about their best friends. I find this especially dark behavior. I want to see their apartments. Probably lots of framed photos of them grinning and squinting next to actors like Ben Affleck, who they met once on the *Armageddon* junket. When people come over they say things like, "Ben's a sweetheart. So down-to-earth. Much nicer than Bruce."

Director Curtis Hanson brings up the rear of the interview hour but they probably should have brought him in first, so fidgety is the assembled group, eager to break for lunch. He's bright, amiable, film-obsessed, funny, and cool. He's asked what it's like to work with Michael Douglas.

Other stuff that happens:

1. Shopping for a new jacket to wear to the Los Angeles Film Critics Awards dinner with Morocco Mole, something that will make me look like the tastiest arm candy ever. "What size do you wear?" asks the salesdude at Neiman Marcus. We're back there because, again, the thrifts don't carry Herman Munster sizes. Ever. And we have a store card now. They only take cash, American Express, or their own card. It's how they force you to open a store account. It's evil.

"I take a 48 or 50, depending."

"Ohhh," he says. "None of our lines really go above 46. You might try a big-and-tall store."

I buy the dangerous dinner plates instead.

2. I have the genuine pleasure of meeting Sonia, who runs the burger stand around the block from my apartment. The stand is called Irv's. It's been around since 1950 and it's showing its age. Sonia is the new proprietor and she's quick to love everyone. She's Korean. She knows every customer's name and their favorite thing to order. She writes it down before you say it. If time permits she'll sing to you and make sure your name appears in the song somewhere.

When your burger is ready she'll write a note on your paper plate or to-go bag with a Sharpie. I introduce myself and my first-ever order comes with a note that reads, "Just for our Dave!" Scientists should study this woman to see if her happiness vibrations could cure chronic illness.

BOTULISM

COME THE END of a year, if you look in the newspaper and bother to read the critic's blurbs in all the Oscar-needy movies and you see the words "WINNER—Best Actress: L.A. Film Critics Association," that means that Morocco Mole and a bunch of other people voted and they gave that award to whoever. LAFCA is a crankier bunch than, say, the people who give out the Golden Globes, and that's why you'll usually notice that the winners are actors you've never heard of from movies you haven't seen yet. Robin Williams tends to get shut out.

Then they have this dinner where the winners show up to get their award plaque and their asses kissed in a pump-priming way before the big rim job of the Golden Globes/ Directors Guild/Writers Guild/Screen Actors Guild/Academy Awards season begins. And I'm there with Morocco. Our ticket says "33" on it. It's our table number, far off to the right-hand side of the hotel banquet room, in the back. Our dinner companions are mostly PR flunkies from the independent arm of a major studio. In other words, no pressure. Thank God we're nonentities or we'd have to make dinner chat with Russell Crowe.

The fashion component is the most interesting part of the evening. Lots of mildly bitter middle-aged film critics and lots of movie stars and lots of tightly wound publicists all carrying giant tote bags. And if you didn't know what any of the famous people looked like, you'd still know who did what for a living from the clothes. Bad hair for lots of the critics. Suits that a high-school shop teacher might wear to church. Sansabelts. Rockports. Morocco, on the other hand, comes correct in a black Calvin Klein suit. He looks so good I want to sex him up in public. Chloe Sevigny and Hilary Swank both arrive in fancy halter tops and trousers. Matt Stone and Trey Parker look like gay rock stars. Trey Parker is wearing intentionally ugly white pants with red Chinese characters all over them.

We're served food. Room-temperature, botulism-daring chicken. Bread that no one touches except me and Morocco. I'm not afraid to ask for the butter.

Then the actual awards part. One after one, critics trudge to the podium and drone on about the stirring, moving, thrilling performances these artists have given. But to listen to them speak, you'd be forgiven for thinking they were giving an oral book report in the dentist's office. A couple of the bores even read their own material straight from the program book. Unable to speak extemporaneously, still they volunteer to get up in front of a crowd and sweat it out. I turn to Morocco, "It's hot in here. Plus, I have a bedtime that must be adhered to and these loads are robbing me of precious sleep."

Morocco: "Behave."

I lean in to whisper a secondary complaint but before I can reach his ear, he's got his mouth near mine, whispering, "Oh yeah, and eat shit, faggot."

I whisper back, "That was the chicken."

Russell Crowe, in accepting his award for *The Insider*,

complains about the cash bar.

The dinner eaten, the awards passed out, the crowd's sleeping asses finally roused and vertical, Morocco chases down Pedro Almodovar. Morocco's Spanish heritage—he's the American-born seventh child of a Basque father and a Madrid-born mother—means that he has it over the monolinguals in the room. He catches up to the fuzzy-haired director and tells him, *en español*, how the man's movies changed his life. That's touching and all, but I can't hang out one more minute with this bunch. I wander to the lobby for some air. Chloe Sevigny's already beat me out there. She's hanging out alone, fumbling through a small clutch purse. Then she pulls out a camera and aims it straight for the autograph vultures and small crowd of paparazzi waiting outside. These folks are literally banging on the glass shouting "Chloe! Chloe!" and holding up eight-by-ten glossies from *Kids*, begging her to step outside and sign them. Her response is to stand in front of the glass and snap off a round of film, capturing them trying to capture her. This pisses them off and makes them shout and bang even more loudly. I feel lucky to be witnessing this, yet I have a hard time understanding why they want her so badly. She's barely famous as it is. If you want to see her in person you can go down to the end of my block and watch for her going into the Flowering Tree veg restaurant to pick up her to-go order.

If she were Goldie Hawn there'd be an assistant fetching that tempeh burger. This is speculative hounding. If she's nominated for an Oscar her autograph price will go up, and then if she's really smart she'll sign everything and glut the market. After that happens they'll leave her alone.

Other stuff that happens:

1. I learn that not only is my writing class being canceled—the Japanese partying continues unabated—but that I'm supposed to organize a field trip for my conversation class. A field trip. For adults.

2. Morocco introduces me to my new favorite tourist spot, the La Brea Tar Pits. When I was a kid, I'd hear Johnny Carson joke about them on "The Tonight Show" but I never quite understood what they were. But now I know. They are pools of tar. The main pit is like a small pond of black ooze. Giant bubbles of air formed deep down in the tar rise up and burst on the surface. It smells like you'd think a pit of tar smells like. The fumes could give a normal person a headache. Birds steer clear of the surface. Best of all, it borders the Los Angeles County Museum of Art's sculpture garden, the enormous concrete Donald Judd cubes teetering on the edge of disaster, waiting for their turn to be engulfed by tar when the next big earthquake ruptures the ground.

3. Morocco also introduces me to Roscoe's Chicken and Waffles of Tapeheads *and 2Pac fame. It's fried chicken and waffles. You eat them together and you're very full when you finish. It has rearranged my tongue's entire way of tasting the world. LL Cool J was there. The LAFCA chiefs need to get these folks to cater next year's dinner.*

PATHETIC

I'M WATCHING A man masturbate.

I don't know his name.

He's my neighbor. He lives across the street.

I've woken early, 6:00 A.M. as usual, my body refusing to believe that I'm a freelancer now. In the words of new friend Vinny, boyfriend of Sean, befriended at the Danielson Famile/Low show, who wears those square indie-rock male librarian glasses as though he were the first person to do so, and who further claims to have invented the cool-kid enclave of Silverlake: "You belong to the night now, fool! Get out of your gaytarded pajamas, take the fucking Sleepytime fucking chamomile tea out of your butt, and become a grown-ass man and be free. Shit."

But I belong to the morning and there's nothing I can do about it. My pattern is fixed. At 9:00 P.M. I begin to fall asleep, and it doesn't really matter where I am, so it kind of helps if that place is home in bed, just to make it easier for everyone. My body thinks I still have to be awake, fresh and ready to teach first period at 7:30 A.M. My body is stupid.

My neighbor's body, on the other hand, is exceptional. I may have a religious preference for a bulkier brand of man, but I don't hate the lean and muscular. This guy's abs stand out at fifty yards, which is roughly the distance between us, me sipping green tea on my balcony in a flannel robe—it's

still sort of chilly outside, being February-ish—and he standing in briefs on his own balcony. Then the briefs disappear
and his abs cease to be as interesting as before.

I suppose if I were living in a different part of the world,
this guy's self-gratification and exhibitionism would be considered perverted and criminal. He is, after all, acting out
sexually without getting my consent. I didn't even nod or
make any gesture that I was ready for an early morning jack-
off show. And what do I know? Maybe moving into West
Hollywood itself is an act of consent. He's not hurting me, in
any case. He's just making himself feel good. He wants me to
share his happiness. So I keep watching and sipping my tea.
At least he's being quiet. If the "whooo" girls would take up
silent public masturbation they'd be a lot less annoying.

I imagine running into this guy at our neighborhood supermarket and sharing a secret smile about our "encounter."
I wonder if I should go wake up Morocco Mole so he can
watch too. (I know better. He comes from a long line of
grumpy-in-the-morning people. He barely acknowledges I
exist before noon.) I wonder what this guy does for a living
and how his co-workers would react if they knew he was
giving the whole world a lap dance right now. I like to think
on the surface he's an upstanding, vaguely uptight GLAAD
employee who makes the world safe for positive gay role
models by day and then lies in a trough at sex clubs at night
so strangers can pee on him, and because of this fantasy I
have a sudden urge to be his friend.

He finishes up, the aftermath leaping over his balcony's
edge and down to the grass below. I give him a thumbs-up
sign and he waves back. Then he disappears into his apartment. The best part of it all is that it made me forget that

green tea really tastes like shit.

"Why didn't you wake me up?" asks Morocco.

"I figured you'd be annoyed if I woke you. You thought I was making up that little earthquake. That sort of set the tone for what was appropriate to bother you about."

"Yeah, you're right."

"I mean, to me, hot neighbors who spank it for breakfast are more important than tiny seismological spasms, so I *would* have woken you," I say. "So you decide. I just want to be a good husband."

"Yeah, fuggit. Let me sleep."

"So my neighbor across the street masturbated on his balcony this morning," I tell Eeyore Ed at ESL school.

"Oh my God! Did you call the police?" he says.

"No, why?"

"You should have. He might be a rapist or something."

"I'm pretty sure this guy isn't a rapist. I think he's just a show-off," I say.

"Still. I can't believe you didn't call!" Ed is more upset than any reasonable person would be. "Did he know you saw him?"

"Oh yes. He acknowledged my presence and kept going."

"And you did nothing! Then you're a pervert too," says Ed, but something tells me he's going to use this story in one of his go-nowhere scripts.

"I'd have taken his picture," says Sean, later that day. "Then I'd post it online. You want an audience? I've got a fucking audience for you. Did he have a big dong?"

"Very," I say. "I could make it out easily even at that distance."

"Then definitely a picture. What were you thinking by

not getting some pictures?"

"All we have is a Spice Girls 'Spice-Cam' Polaroid."

"You're making that up," says Vinny.

"No, I'm not. It's a Polaroid. You know, it spits out the picture and then it develops before your eyes. Only ours is pink and it says 'Spice-Cam' on it and there are little stickers of Baby and Sporty and Scary and Posh and Ginger. The pictures come out kinda blurry. We bought it at Kmart just as the Spice Girls were breaking up. It was on sale."

"You're fucking pathetic for not using it," says Vinny.

Other stuff that happens:

1. I interview up-and-coming-fashion designer Rick Owens for Glue. *I write the piece. It never runs.*

2. For the fashion website, I interview a woman who's been a Hollywood hairstylist since the early 1960s. She did Barbra Streisand's hair for her first appearance on "The Judy Garland Show." She helped create Farrah's famously feathered and blown-out "Charlie's Angels" head. She worked on Michelle Pfeiffer when she was Catwoman. She remembers it being very cold on the set because of all the penguins. After I write it, the story is killed. I get a check anyway, feel hollow inside, cash it, and buy a new pair of boots.

3. Thanks to my Glue affiliation, a Dutch fashion and style magazine called, appropriately enough, Dutch, *contacts me about interviewing Paul Verhoeven. I'm a huge fan of his early Dutch movies and a stalwart defender of* Showgirls *and* Starship Troopers *as art films whose times have yet to come. Then I try to get through to him. He's shooting* Hollow Man *so that's tough. Meanwhile, none of his people have heard of* Dutch, *and they can't quite get their* heads around the fact that it's a Dutch magazine published in Paris and written in English. I'm bumped from the studio's domestic to international publicity offices and back again, referred by assistants to higher-ups who never call back, told by multiple people over the course of the same call that he's not doing press at the moment and also that he'd probably like the idea of doing something for a Dutch magazine. I mail copies of the magazine to everyone who asks for one. I'm ping-ponged between no and maybe so often I lose track of who said what. Then Dutch kills the story.

4. Just when I'm feeling like my life is stalling again, Morocco brings home free tickets to see Sally Kellerman perform her one-woman show in the Valley, free passes to an American Cinematheque screening of Mandingo, and news that Diamanda Galas is coming to town. It's Christmas again.

VILE

"DUDE, WHERE ARE you going?" I ask Morocco Mole. "You should just turn right here on Hollywood Boulevard, because Franklin is no faster on a Sunday afternoon."

Morocco, who already has his preferred route picked out and catalogued in his mind regardless of that route's efficacy, says, "Oh, Señor Mappy has directions?"

Then I explain to him that in my limited experience I have found that going to Los Feliz is faster on Fountain during the week but on the weekend it doesn't make a difference whether you take any east/west street, Fountain or Hollywood or Sunset or Franklin, and that, in fact, Hollywood or Sunset are probably the fastest of all on the weekend—days, not nights, because then Sunset is a parking lot of desperate teenage lovedolls from Granada Hills who just come over the hill to drink with fake IDs, fuck shit up, and get preggers. But then there's the part where that little stretch of Hollywood Boulevard gets all touristy, so that's another consideration. I always take Fountain. Just because I do.

"Guess what you are now?" asks Morocco.

"What's that?" I say.

"An *Angeleeeeno!*"

"Oh really? Guess, then, what my new Angeleno superpower is," I say.

"What?"

"Shut the fuck up."

"Hmm. Yeah, that's a real burn."

But here is the faulty logic of Morocco Mole: Since driving is all anyone does here, having routes to places in my head and not varying from them makes me a citizen, or, in my case, means that I've passed my first round of citizenship tests. He's grasping at any straw he can to convince me that I will learn to call this place home, that time plus the cumulative wear and tear of being hurried along by a city that moves about a hundred miles an hour faster than what I'm used to will eventually engender affection. He means well. He wants me to feel his civic pride.

"Assimilation is not a preferred traffic route," I say.

"Tell me about three places here that you love," he says.

"I haven't been programmed to love, only to punch," I say, holding up my fist to his nose.

"Do it," he says. I tap his nose gently with my fist. I talk all tough. Plus he's driving. So I tell him that I really like Canter's Deli because they have a beautiful ceiling and because Rodney on the ROQ has his own booth there. I also like the 99¢ Store because you can get 99¢ lunch meat there that you have to eat really really fast or it'll expire before you get it in between the bread slices, and because their mesmerizing, neatly-arranged product-repetition window displays are a visual tab of Ecstasy. And I like the house on Fairfax with the neon sign on top that says "Asthma Vapineze." I wish I knew what goes on inside.

Suddenly, the car in the lane to our right decides to make a U-turn from his lane, cutting us off and nearly causing us to smash into his driver's side.

"HOLY FUCK!" shouts Morocco Mole, as the other driver screeches oncoming traffic to a frightening halt in his attempt to die young. Even more inexplicably, we see him in our rearview mirror change his mind about it all and do another U-turn which eventually leaves him back where he started, right next to us in traffic at a stop light. He's one of the Dress-All-Stupid Queens, wearing one of those little stripy shirts that Banana Republic can't keep in stock for all the cocksuckers lined up to wear one home, peroxide hair scorching his head. He's talking on his phone and dancing in his seat to La Bouche's "Be My Lover." Now, by telling you this I'm not saying that house music is the internationally recognized sound-signifier of the faggot douchebag, but there's a very specific type of faggot douchebag who *only* listens to house music, and so as a genre it's a little guilty by association. Kind of like how hip-hop equals murder and crime, and country equals believing in Creationism. But the real lesson of this encounter is, once again, that it doesn't matter who you terrify or nearly kill, as long as you get what you want.

"ASSHOLE!" yells Morocco.

La Bouche, however, is bumping too loudly for La Douche to hear Morocco's bellow.

Morocco looks at me. Then turns back to the driver and yells, "YOU HAVE A VERY SMALL PENIS!"

"Dang, I wish he could hear you," I say. Then the light turns green and La Douche takes his La Bouche and speeds off. "Catch up with him again," I say. "Let me get in an 'Eat shit, faggot.'"

But it's too late. La Douche runs the next red.

Other stuff that happens:
1. I decide to take the Weetzie Bat *tour of L.A. I don't know why I didn't think of it before. Francesca Lia Block's book about a*

teenage punk rock girl who sees Los Angeles through rose-colored glasses is one of my favorite fairy tales and it's full of real-life locations that I figure I have to experience. I may feel like a black pit of weepy steel-guitar home-longing, but I'm getting fed up with my own bullshit. First stop on the Weetzie Walk: Oki Dog. At Oki Dog you order the Oki Dog and what you get is a hot dog covered in chili and onions and pastrami and beans and wrapped in a tortilla. It will kill you instantly. Actor Craig comes with me.

"This is vile," he says after taking his first bite. Then he takes an even bigger second bite.

"I know," I say, "Isn't it delicious? Darby Crash used to hang out at this place."

"I can't come back here," says Craig. "If I die too young I'll only be remembered for Kiss Me Guido."

So yeah, Oki Dog is a dump—the grossest, tastiest fast-food hut I've ever been in. But I'm undaunted. If it's good enough for a fictional character and a dead rock star then it's good enough for me. There's a sign in the window that says only, "CHOP CHOP!" An Oki Dog mystery.

2. The field trip for adults is coming up. I still don't get why this is happening. Adults can take themselves anywhere they feel like going. I'd just as soon call in sick that day. But still, I ask my class what they'd like to do on the special day.

"Stay here," says Frenchie lesbo Charlotte. "I don't understand why we are doing this."

"Well," I say, "maybe it will be something you've never done, something specifically American that you haven't experienced yet." This is as much fake enthusiasm as I can muster. I'm not being paid enough to manufacture more.

"I do many things," Charlotte goes on. "And I can do them after *class. In class I want you to be here teaching."*

One of the Korean housewives pipes up, "Do we receive a grade for that day?"

"Um...no."

The smirks on their faces turn to smiles, then to open laughter.

"Just make sure you don't exceed your absence limit."

I've just given them all permission to skip school. I'm going to be fired.

DAMN

"DID YOU KNOW Sally Kellerman sang?" asks Morocco.

"I didn't know she was still alive," I said. Which is kind of a lie. I know who she is, I know she's older than my mom, I know she's not dead yet, and I know she starred in the original Robert Altman film version of *MASH* as Hot Lips. I know she was in this terrifically awful musical version of *Lost Horizon* soon after. I know she did commercial voice-overs for FDS and Hidden Valley Ranch salad dressing. But apart from remembering her songs in *Lost Horizon*, which was nearly thirty years ago, I didn't know she was a person who'd get up on a stage and sing for a crowd. But here we are, at the El Portal Center for the Arts in North Hollywood, about to witness her one-woman show called "Hot Lips."

We find seats and scope out the crowd, all of them dressed in that way that normal people dress when they decide it's an elegant night out on the town. Most of the audience is middle-aged heterosexual couples. Men in pleated Dockers, the ladies in floral skirts and matching jackets with padded shoulders. There's one guy in a baby-blue T-shirt featuring a marijuana leaf decal on the front. It reads, "Weed of Wisdom."

"I gotta go talk to that dude," I say to Morocco.

"Sit still," he whispers.

The tickets say 8:00 P.M. but by 8:20 Sally hasn't hit the stage yet. Why is she making us wait? Morocco leans in and says, "They're backstage pouring black coffee down her throat right now."

Then, as if in rebellion to his slander, Sally bounds onto the stage. She's tall, she's thin, she's got on sky-high heels to make her eight-foot-long legs appear to be nine. And she begins to sing, sing, and sing.

Sally sings the "W-O-M-A-N" song about bringing home the bacon and frying it up in the pan; she sings "Don't You Feel My Leg" and "You and Me against the World." She does between-song patter about Marlon Brando hitting on her once and how she turned him down. She talks about keeping fit by "walking up and down these damn hills" and by regular Pilates. She whips out slides of her kids and husband and sings "Damn Your Eyes" to a giant projection of her man's, yes, eyes.

And then a quick costume change before launching into the centerpiece of the act: a mind-blowing tribute medley to female songwriters that begins with songs from the present and works backwards in time.

A partial set list. Sally's commentary in parentheses.

"Music of My Heart." ("Diane Warren has written so much beautiful music for films, don't you think?")

"I Feel Lucky." ("Ahh, Mary Chapin Carpenter.")

"Nick of Time." ("Ahh, Bonnie Raitt.")

"I'm So Excited." ("And then the eighties with the Pointer Sisters!")

"That's What Friends Are For"/"The Way We Were"/"Gonna Fly Now."

"I Feel the Earth Move." ("Ahh, Carole King.") I whisper

to Morocco, "Carole King, that feminist, also co-wrote 'He Hit Me and It Felt Like a Kiss.'"

"Wedding Bell Blues." ("Ahh, the brilliant Laura Nyro.")

"Stand by Your Man."

"We Shall Overcome." ("Ahh, Zilphia Horton. She really said it for us all, didn't she?")

"Young at Heart."

"How High the Moon," during which Morocco leans in to me: "Not as high as this medley."

"God Bless the Child."

"Who's Afraid of the Big Bad Wolf?"

"America, the Beautiful."

And the grand finale, "The Battle Hymn of the Republic." When it ends, Sally salutes and the "Theme from *MASH*" kicks in. Good night, North Hollywood.

We walk back to the car in silence. "What did we just watch?" asks Morocco in the car.

"I will tell you," I say. "That show was about how you can be sixtysomething and still trot around all horsey in Manolo Blahniks and fucking sing medleys and be self-indulgently slinky and just do whatever you want no matter how dorky it is. Because really, who was waiting for that show to happen tonight? That would be no-fucking-body. The cats who make the entertainment decisions for America couldn't give a rat's ass about Sally Kellerman because she's the age when most actresses are fed up and saying, 'Fuck this shit, I'm gonna go do some animal charities and bake a pie.' This is her saying, 'Look motherfuckers, I'll plant my own tree. I wanna sing the motherfucking 'Battle Hymn of the Republic!'"

"And you couldn't have seen that in Texas," adds Morocco. I really hate it when he says this. And he's doing it a lot lately, pointing out all of the city's superior cultural opportunities.

"Don't fuck with me," I snap. "Texas has Betty Buckley."

Other stuff that happens:

1. We have another new neighbor. A drug dealer. This particular drug dealer has naturally wavy dark brown hair all the way down his back, never wears a shirt, and stands outside of the apartment building across the street, strumming an unplugged electric guitar all day. Cars drive up, he chats with them for a moment, there's an exchange of goods, the car drives off. Every other day or so, if I'm at my kitchen window doing dishes and admiring his chest, he'll catch me looking. Then he'll grin and nod. One day I make pancakes for breakfast and he must smell the bacon frying. Finally he speaks for the first time: "Hey man. Good morning."

I wave back.

"You makin' breakfast, man?"

I nod, then silently kick myself because now he might want to invite himself up. Not that I could be so cruel as to deny my friendly neighborhood pusher-man some of my really delicious pancakes, but I'm afraid that if he comes into our apartment he might just be casing the joint instead of truly paying attention to my special flair with buttermilk.

"Whatcha makin'?"

"Pancakes," I say, somewhat timidly, because I'm still sort of nervous about his intentions. High people always make me a little nervous.

"Mmmmm, good," he says, rubbing his belly, his belly that hasn't been destroyed by overly fastidious ab-cultivation, the one that's making me horny and I can't believe I'm hot for the neighborhood drug dealer. I snap out of it when he gets into his car, turns up the

Freedom Rock, and speeds away.

    2. The adult field trip—to the local bowling alley—comes and goes without a hitch. Five of my fifteen students show up, which is more than I expected. The office manager says to me, "Where are your students?"
    "I don't know. Maybe smoking under the bleachers."
    "What?"
    "Nothing."
    "You did not tell them to come?"
    "Yes. I did."
    "But not enough."
    "I can't make them do anything."
    "You must stress the importance of the school."
    "Right. I'm on it."

    3. Celebrity sighting: Drew Barrymore and Tom Green. They're arm in arm, walking down Hollywood Boulevard late at night. Her head is down but his isn't—like it would have mattered since he's such a big tall gork. This is the sort of thing that tourists the world over think they're going to see when they come to Hollywood Boulevard. But they never do. I resist the urge to tell Drew I have weird psychological dreams about her tits.

4

DEPRESSION
April & May

LUMP

MOROCCO MOLE HAS shaved his head. Not cut it short. Shaved it all off in a fetishy, ritualistic way. A little late in life, perhaps, for this sort of skull experimentation, but he'd been jonesing to do it forever, so he finally stepped up to the plate. I don't have the heart to tell him he looks like Uncle Fester now. So I get Tom Ford to tell him for me. I shaved my own head, back in 1986, my visibly punk-rock years, prompting my younger brother to rename me "Skinhead" and, when forced into a logic corner in any argument, to end that quarrel with, "Oh, brave words from someone who shaves his head to the bone." Anyway, I'm making Morocco use tons of sunblock on his big white Charlie Brown dome because I believe cancer lurks around every corner. And to ward off my own trip to the oncologist, I've adopted a few popular West Hollywood magical health practices. My green tea mornings with the Crystal Meth Queens continue and I've developed head-nod relationships with several of them. They forget from day to day that I'm still not the one who's going to hook them up with either variety of booty bump, but they're polite about it all the same. And I continue to take up space at City Yoga, the little studio about fifteen minutes of walk time from our apartment. I stroll along, mat in hand, soaked in sweat so people can see that I, Fatso, have been exercising, as they think to themselves *Look at him!*

He's got it together! even though I've just spent sixty torture-minutes with my turbaned, knocked-up instructress as she's tried to force me into a headstand, something *she* can do in her sleep but that I can't do with a gun held to my face, resulting in my constant grimace and her chirping, "Find your smile! Aren't you happy?" and to which I respond, "Maybe in the future when I'm done here and eating a doughnut from the shop down the street." Finally, I slather on the sunblock—obsessively, compulsively—and stay out of the death-inducing rays with a zeal previously reserved exclusively for Nick Cave's personal use.

So of course I discover a lump.

I make an appointment with my doctor as quickly as I can, which means I have a four-week wait ahead of me. My panic attack over this won't subside, however, until I get myself into her examination room, so I call each day at 7:00 A.M. until I hit the other-patient-cancellation lotto. This takes eight days.

Once I'm finally there, shirtless and lying on her table, my doctor feels around my upper left pectoral muscle until she hits the lump. "Men can get breast cancer, too, right?" I ask.

"Very good. Most women don't even know about that."

"Quincy Jones had it," I say. "I went online to find out about it."

"Now, I don't want you to get yourself too worked up about this yet," she says, "but in the meantime, without being too alarming, I will say that, yes, it's a possibility that this fibrous mass, and that's all we know about it at the moment, could be something you don't want."

"Right. So when do we take it out? I'm ready right now."

"It doesn't work like that. I'll need to schedule you for a mammogram."

"A what?"

"Do you know what a mammogram is?"

"Yes, but I don't have a mammo to gram."

"Oh yes, you do. I thought you said you read up on this."

"Well, I did, but what will they put in the part that squeezes the breast?"

"Don't worry. They'll know what to put in there."

Later, back at home, Morocco Mole and I are on the couch. I'm resting my head in his lap. "This is most likely nothing, you understand," he says.

"You don't know that. I could be dying right now, as we speak. Wasting away with cancer of the male boob."

"I hardly think you're wasting away," he says, patting my belly.

"I could be riddled with it, shot through with multiple carcinomas. What if it's spread down to my dick? I'll be dickless."

"That would be an adjustment for you," he says, "what with having to find a new place to live and all."

I practice my own version of the Watch How Now I'm Ignoring What You Say look. "This could be eating my brains and spleen and whatever right now. I could have six weeks to live like in that movie with Dudley Moore and Mary Tyler Moore and the little ballet girl who drops dead at Christmas after dancing in *The Nutcracker*."

"Your own death would not be that hilarious to me. But I assume you won't be dancing in *The Nutcracker* anytime soon. So you have nothing to worry about."

Other stuff that happens:

1. Fear of Death record purchases: Merzbow's Venereology, *Bobbie Gentry's* Ode to Billie Joe, *Minutemen's* Double Nickels on the Dime. *I needed it on CD. My vinyl copy is old and beat up because I'm that punk rock.*

2. I go to Rite-Aid to buy a bottle of Phisoderm for Morocco Mole. It's the soap that bald people need to use to cleanse their sensitive scalps. Then back to Fred Segal for some Kiehl's moisturizer with SPF 15. It's pretty expensive but "we" need it now that one of us has shaved his head to the bone.

FUCKFACE

I KNOW THAT the sentence "I have to go to a fancy hotel and interview celebrities" probably inspires less sympathy than, "I have to decide which one of my children to send to the gas chamber," so I expect none. I know, too, that it's good to have something occupying my brain between the interminable stretch of days between lump discovery and lump mammography. And I know that any reason for taking a day off from the increasingly draggy experience of teaching adults who barely need my help and who either skip class entirely or spend their fifty minutes with me massaging each other's uvulas is a good reason. So here I am, stationed in the enormous penthouse suite of a Century City hotel, about to interview celebrities, even though I'd just as soon be home scrubbing bathroom grout. Spiritual Andy is with me. He's already seasoned junket press. He knows how to talk more loudly than the other interviewers to get his question in, he backs down from no one, and he knows how to ask the inappropriate personal questions in a way that makes it seem like the celebrity has, in fact, no other choice but to answer promptly, truthfully, now.

Pre-lump, Morocco and I see the movie I'll be junketeering over. A romantic comedy starring John Cusack set in a struggling indie record shop in Chicago, we both enjoy it enough. We leave the screening room and he's ready with the question I can sense he's about to ask. "You were the Jack Black character, weren't you?" he says, referring to my twelve years of service in three different independent record stores back in Texas.

"I think that depends on what you mean, my darling," I say, coyly.

"I think you know what I mean," he says. "You were the fuckface who turned up your nose when people bought something middlebrow like Stone Temple Pilots."

"Wrong-o," I say. "I was the sensitive fuckface who, *in his mind,* turned up his nose when people bought shit sandwiches by Stone Temple Pilots, but who never once insulted anyone for their consumer choices, even when their favorite band was the sworn enemy of all music. Like Stone Temple Pilots."

"You live in a house of lies."

Andy and I grab heaps of bacon from the breakfast buffet. "Who cares how much we eat?" he reasons. "They did, after all, provide this for us. We might as well take as much as we want."

I'm studying the back of the promo soundtrack CDs we've been given. "Who are the Thirteenth Floor Elevators?" asks Andy. "I don't know who any of the new bands are."

"Thirteenth Floor Elevators aren't new," I say. "They're from the sixties. It's a mix of old and new on here."

"I'm going to hate all this, aren't I?" asks Andy.

"Didn't you pay attention to the music in the movie?"

"Not really."

"Well there's Stevie Wonder at the end. You like him, right?" I say.

"Oh, because I'm black?" snaps Andy.

"Yes. But also because you're out of it. Just like Stevie Wonder."

"Oh my god you are *so* like that Jack Black guy in the movie."

Lisa Bonet is up first to be interviewed. She's one of John Cusack's love interests in the film. She's been taking a little break from Hollywood. Raising her kid. If I were going to accuse someone of being stoned at nine o'clock on a Wednesday morning, she might be the person I'd single out. But then again, she could just be really, really laid back. She sits at the table with the dozen or so radio and online journalists, fielding sleepy toilet-paper-gentle questions. On my pad of paper, I write the following note to Andy: "I'll give you twenty bucks if you can get her to call Lenny Kravitz her 'babydaddy.'"

He writes back, all caps: "MAKE IT 50."

As an admittedly novice and, even more accurately, flat-out lazy junketeer, I sit back and let other people ask the questions. Andy writes to me: "You're not even *trying* to get a question in."

I write back: "I'm too starstruck to talk to Cosby kids."

Andy: "Imposter. Go home to Texas and get back to teaching those middle-school children you abandoned."

Jack Black is next. He's come prepared and sings the words to the *Star Trek* theme song for the assembled bunch without being asked to do so. No one cares why he's doing it. We're just happy he is. I'm nothing like this guy, I just want to state for the record. So I do.

Note to Andy: "I'm nothing like this guy."

Note to me: "You're right. He's successful at what he does."

Note to Andy: "Is it my negative energy that's making you so cruel to me?"

Note to me: "Nope. My own."

Andy's right, though. I am inept at this job. I don't like to bark out questions on top of other people. I don't like to push the famous people into answering irrelevant personal probes. I'm just not interested. I had this fantasy that press junket roundtables would be like something from *La Dolce Vita*, where Anita Ekberg's character answers meaning-of-life questions like "What do you believe in?" with the answer, "Love, love, and love." But this is all, "What drew you to the character?" and there's no fighting the tide. Idiosyncratic, oddball, interesting lines of questioning are seen as a waste of everyone's time. And the celebrities, when they're *not* being asked interesting questions, are bored or bemused, irritated or passive-aggressive. They're here to fulfill the marketing clause in their contract. They'd rather be at a spa getting a colonic. This is a publicity machine to be oiled and we're the mechanics. I learned that my first time out. But I'll do it until something less soul-crushing comes along.

And the soul-crushing continues when John Cusack enters the room. He sits at the table and takes the first question. And when he opens his mouth to speak, he does so at what may very well be a negative level of decibels. Without skipping a beat, every single person around the table stands and moves their tiny tape recorders to the spot on the table closest to him. Otherwise we're all sunk. The publicist hurries to turn off the room's air-conditioning because it's actually drowning him out. No one dares ask him to speak up.

Note to Andy: "Um. What the fuck, John Cusack?!"

Note to me: "Shrug."

Note to Andy: "Does he have a cold? Laryngitis?"

Note to me: "Possibly. But he hates the press. He may just have fuck–all–y'all–itis."

I sit at the table hoping my tape recorder will pick up the actor's barely audible mumble. I think, "You'd better be running a near-death fever, Mr. Brother to Joan Who I Like Better Anyway." Doesn't he understand that I'm not like the other people here? *I'm down with bands like Royal Trux and the Velvet Underground, too John! I think to myself. Just like you! Now speak the fuck up!* John Cusack, however, does not tune into my ESP message.

Other stuff that happens:

1. On the elevator ride down to the lobby, I listen to two male junketeers talk about house-casting. One of them owns a home that has recently been in the running to be used as a location for two different films. Sadly, the house was passed over both times. There's a pause, then I offer that maybe his house needs to lose some weight. This is met with stony silence.

2. Next stop on the Weetzie Bat *tour: Jayne Mansfield's home.*

Being long-dead, she no longer lives there. That's Engelbert Humperdinck's job. To his credit he hasn't changed it from the ditzy pink it's been painted all these years. I stop in front, looking it over, but don't turn off the gas. I'm no loiterer. Jayne's not buried in Los Angeles, but she has a gravestone at the Hollywood Memorial Park Cemetery all the same.

3. Non-junket-related celebrity sighting: Gina Gershon at my local Mobil station, while I wait for my car to be smog-checked. She's traveling incognito with giant Two for the Road *sunglasses and a ratty T-shirt, buying Advil while I try not to stare. She's really tiny, but then they all are here. And the shades are a good move. You don't be Gina Gershon and just gallivant through West Hollywood unshielded. You are Cristal Connors. You are in the best movie ever. You will be mobbed. But for the record, I do not mob. I'd had enough fame in my face for one day.*

DIE

I'VE DECIDED TO adopt the calm yoga-dude approach to my lump. I've decided that if Quincy Jones can get cancer in his man-teat and not die, then so can I. I, after all, do not have the added stress of Michael Jackson or Peggy Lipton in my life. I'm going to live, just like Q. And when I finally beat this lump into submission I'm going to quit that fucking teaching job.

Meanwhile, though, I have to return to the big HMO compound for an appointment with my allergist. I'm bad at breathing. My lungs hate me. They also hate Los Angeles's brand of air. In Texas they hated the Texas plants and Texas grasses and Texas trees. In Los Angeles it's Los Angeles plants and grasses and trees and Linda Hunt almost running me down at a traffic stop across the street from my allergist's office. This is my third near-miss moment with a moving car, and it turns out to be a car driven by an Oscar winner. She slams on her brakes to avoid running a standing red light just as I'm crossing the street. She's not the tallest of ladies and her face is somewhat obscured by the steering wheel, so I have to look twice to make sure it's her. It's her. She gives me the wave and mouths the word, "Sorry."

My allergist's office is located on the third floor of a building in my HMO's complex. I get off the elevator and enter what can only be someone's birthday party at the appointment desk. The radio's up loud, Gloria Estefan singing some horrible ballad, the people behind the desk animated and chatty. They seem to know all the patients in line by name. I have no fucking idea what's going on. Maybe there are people who like to hang out at hospital appointment desks now. Maybe it's this whole new party scene that I'll eventually read about in the style section of the *Los Angeles Times*, long after the originators have moved on to newer, hipper spots.

I check in, see my allergist—she's changing my prescription to something stronger—and leave. It's a simple visit, but now I have a choice. I can go to the Rite-Aid near my house, be done in less than thirty minutes, and pay full price, or I can go to the HMO molasses-factory pharmacy and grow old there. I opt for molasses, drop off my prescription at the check-in station and sit down. A man with a big boil on his head sits next to me. Two minutes later a woman knitting something sits on my other side. She smells like day-old cooked broccoli. I quietly get up to move. When I get to my new seat, I look back at her and she's scowling at me. She reeks but she's the one who gets to be offended. In my new spot, I watch a grandmother teaching a toddler all the wrong words to the patty-cake rhyme. He's going to end up in a preschool fistfight with some kid who knows the actual words.

I wait for forty-five minutes. It's no problem really. I have a Dawn Powell book to keep me company in anticipation of this very thing, but it's hard to concentrate on reading because there are a lot of people with crazy ailments, hacking, grinding lung expulsions, limps, and bandaged wounds to fascinate on. Boil on Head Man is especially intriguing. I'd have stayed closer to him if it weren't for stenchy Lady

Broccoli. Then the LED board on the wall flashes my name. That's my cue to go stand in a very long pick-up line for another unknown amount of time. The line stretches out the pharmacy door and eliminates my ability to see. Back to reading. Just then a man walks out with his prescription and yells, "Y'ALL ARE GONNA BE IN THAT LINE FOR TWO MORE HOURS! HA HA HA! SUMMA Y'ALL GONNA DIE BEFORE YOU GET THAT MEDICINE! HA!"

Other stuff that happens:

1. I end up having to go to Rite-Aid anyway. We're out of mouthwash. I'm in line behind Danny Bonaduce. He's wearing sweatpants and buying a gallon of milk. Then Ethan Hawke stands in line behind me. He smells like an ashtray. I know about the whole smoking killing your sense of smell thing, but dang, Ethan Hawke, get a fucking personal assistant whose job it is to inform you that you have nicotine funk coming out your pores.

2. I turn in my piece about the John Cusack junket. My editor says, "These are great quotes you got."

"It was nothing," I say.

3. The police cart off Shirtless Drug Dealer Guy. It's a big early evening ordeal. I stand on our apartment balcony and watch. He goes quietly, a smile on his face. He even looks up at one point, sees me watching, and then nods to me like we're buds. Now a lot of his regulars are going to have to find a new connection. If I'd only talked to "Weed of Wisdom" guy at the Sally Kellerman show and maybe gotten his number, I could call him and tell him there's an opening on our block.

4. *I feel romantic and buy Morocco a love gift:* Pills-a-Go-Go: A Fiendish Investigation into Pill Marketing, Art, History & Consumption. *He's excited. Morocco has more than a casual interest in* Valley of the Dolls. *It would not be going too far to say that he's obsessed with it. Typical gay, yes, but at least when he goes around quoting it he's more likely to sample a less-repeated line from the movie, such as, "It was not a nuthouse!" or even something from the book about Tony Polar having rough anal sex with Jennifer North.*

PAIN

I LIKE THE idea of having part of me in a vise. I know
that when it happens I'll most likely change my tune, but
there's something about my upcoming mammogram that has
me fantasizing that I'm going to be in a David Cronenberg
movie, darkly celebrating the fusion of flesh and machine. I
tell friends this over Sunday pancakes. We're listening to Dot-
tie West. I think of it as a good litmus to see which of these
friends, both the new and the ones that I inherited with the
purchase of Morocco's soul, is worth keeping. Morocco says,
"I like to think of whatever pain you feel during that moment as just desserts for all the times you've rolled over in
your sleep and elbowed me in the face."

"Will you cry?" asks Tom Ford. "Because I hear that's
what you do first."

"And if you cry can I take pictures?" asks Vinny's boyfriend Sean.

"Make sure if it bruises his tit and turns it all black and
blue to get a shot of that, too," adds Vinny.

"I volunteer to gently caress the not-mammogrammed
nipple," says Dave 2.

"And I'll rub soothing creams, lotions, and salves on the
wrecked one," says Morocco.

They all pass the test.

It's the day. I enter the waiting room, walk up to the window, and drop off my check-in forms. "May I help you?" asks the woman behind the desk.

"I'm just dropping these off," I say. She gives me a mildly surprised look, then glances down at the papers, adjusts her face, and says "Okay, have a seat."

There are seven women seated nearby. I can feel the side-long glances and the unabashedly indignant stares. I'm the lone man, the creepy fat guy who just showed up to pee all over the furniture of their "safe space." *Yes, bitches,* I think to myself, *I got no business being here. I'm only hanging out so maybe I can sneak a peek or cop a feel of your lumpy tits. That's why I brought this book with me, to throw you off.* I imagine the mammo-givers standing around in the back fighting over who has to deal with squashing my fat into the boob-press, drawing little pink straws and saying, "Nuh-uh! *You* do it!" My name is called and fourteen eyes follow my every step out.

I enter the testing room (sign on wall: "WE COM-PRESS BECAUSE WE CARE") and the Mammo Tech Lady, who seems more bored than resentful of my presence, tells me to take off my shirt, then to push my chest up to the cold metal shelf where my breast will be mashed. This is where it gets problematic. I'm a fat dude but I'm not the sort of super-chub who has serious moobs. I don't know exactly how I'm supposed to get my chest-fat onto a slab that's ob-viously designed for someone more jugsy. "You don't have much to work with, do you?" asks Mammo Tech Lady.

"No, I guess not. Sorry." I've just apologized for not being even fatter than I already am. I want her to like me.

That's when she reaches for my chest and begins to knead and pull as much of my fat as she can onto the shelf. "You're going to have to squeeze as much of your chest as you can," she instructs. "Do it where the mass is located and try to shape it into something more like a breast so whatever it is you have can be seen."

I do as she says. The cold metal machine's squeezy cold metal action begins. My vise fantasy was not inaccurate. Imagine having your blood pressure tested and multiply that by ten. Imagine total pain. I say, "Hey. This hurts."

"Yes," says Mammo-Tech Lady, "it does."

Next, ultrasound. I'm taken into another room, where I lie down next to a small TV screen. Other Tech Lady breaks out the ultrasound gloop and rubs it on the left side of my chest. The next few minutes are spent with me on my back, having my lump prodded with a stick. Anything unusual is supposed to show up on the TV screen. I watch the static-filled monitor, hoping to see a glowing orb or a fetus or something exciting. But there's nothing. My lump, it's mysterious.

I wait a week for the results. My chest still hurts but I don't have even a half-assed decent bruise to show for it.

Other stuff that happens:

1. I'm not in the mood for my first-ever movie premiere but it happens anyway. A movie that should forever remain nameless because it wasn't worth the effort to screen for the press. Morocco calls this "burying." This may not be the precise technical term, but it's something studios do when they're ashamed of the movie and think it not worth the effort to promote. Because most major studio films have 50 percent of their take—or something like that—in the first weekend, the studio hopes to have a middling-to-decent opening weekend at the box-office by not letting the press see it. By the time the reviews hit the papers on Sunday or Monday, it's no big whoop what the critics think. But for some reason, when I call the publicist to ask about screenings, she says, "We're not having critic's screenings," but then adds, "but you're with IFILM.com right? You can just go to the premiere."

Does this mean IFILM is someone they like? Does it mean that Internet movie reviews are so worthless it doesn't matter who they let in? I don't have the luxury of caring either way, really. I've already come to understand that questioning any publicist is a sucker's move. Why they do what they do is as mysterious as my lump. All I know is that this is a check I still get to earn, so I ask what time I need to be there.

When I arrive my name isn't on the list.

"Who are you with," says the gay male publicist—again, the Gay Voice, plus he's a Dress-All-Stupid Queen in a faux-vintage cowboy shirt. There's no question mark at the end of his sentence. He's asking me a question but it's delivered in the world-weariest of tones, soaking me in disdain. He doesn't care who I'm with. He's upset that I haven't dressed for the occasion. My T-shirt, jeans, boots, notebook, and extra book to read while killing time ensemble is getting a big thumbs-down. I'm clearly unimportant, but am I unimportant enough for him to let through the rope without getting fired for doing it?

"Who's your contact," he asks again, flatly.

I tell him the name of the publicist. "I'm writing that down," he warns. And then I'm in. Sort of. I try to walk in the side door but a cement-block wall of a security guard stops me. "Hold it, you can't go in this door. You have to walk up the carpet to the main door."

I look at the red carpet. A hundred photographers line each side, ready for fresh famous meat to strut past their blinding flashes. "Oh, you're shitting me. I have to walk through over there?"

"Yes sir," Cement Wall announces impatiently.

Suddenly I'm not wearing a T-shirt and jeans. I'm naked. I take a deep breath and hold my head down so all I see is red carpet, I move as quickly as my feet will take me. I hear one photographer ask another, "Who's that?"

I hear the other one respond, "Nobody."

"Who brings a book to a movie premiere?" asks the woman about to sit in front of me. I've stationed myself in the very last row of the theater in the farthest aisle seat. I want out as quickly as possible when the credits begin to roll. And I'm reading my book.

"I do," I say.

She's wearing a cowboy hat and sparkly blouse. She's grinning at me. She looks sort of familiar but I can't place her. "What book is it?" she says, taking it out of my hand. I'm going to slug this bitch.

"Dawn Powell," I say.

"Who's that?" she asks, excited, like I'm going to tell her about the greatest thing she's ever heard of in her life. My urge to slug diminishes. I'm starting to dig her a little bit.

"Dawn Powell was the Dorothy Parker nobody's ever heard of," I say.

"Ooh, I'll have to go get one of her books!" says Cowboy Hat Lady. "Why are you here with this book? Did you" (lowering her voice to a stage whisper) "sneak in?"

"I'm a movie critic," I say, which for tonight is the truth.

"Ooooh, a critic. I'm an actress," says Cowboy Hat Lady. That's where I've seen her, in stuff.

"You know what?" I say, "I think I've seen you somewhere."

"Ooooh, where?!"

"Well back when I lived in Texas I think I saw you in a Tetley Iced Tea Commercial. You were bothered by the fact that the tea bag was round."

Suddenly, she's mock-outraged. "Young man," she says haugh-

tily, "I'll have you know that I am a soap opera diva!"

"Really?"

"Yes, do you watch 'Days of Our Lives'?"

"Not since summer vacation of 1977," I say.

"Well, I'm on 'Days,' honey. An iced tea commercial, indeed," she huffs, laughing. "Everything I've done and you know me from a tea commercial."

What's your name?" I ask.

"Patrika," she says, "Darbo. Who are you?"

"Dave White."

"Nice to meet you, Dave. Now give me your pen so I can write down the name of that book."

2. I'm about to put wet clothes into a dryer at Launderland— home of Transylvania's finest male prostitutes—when a woman yells at me to stop because there's food in the dryers. She yells this five times in a row. As entertainments go, she's no Patrika Darbo.

FAILURE

IN THE TWENTY-FOUR hours since the Tech Ladies got their hands on my mammary glands, I've done my best to imagine my yesterday as just another kinky sex act I needed to explore. I got a sensitive body part crushed by a machine, then I got rubbed with something that felt like lube, and poked with what could have doubled as a vibrator. So compared to Julie Christie getting impregnated by a satanic rape-computer in *Demon Seed*, I had it easy.

And regardless of the outcome, I've decided to quit the teaching job. I'm already bored. No one in the class really needs my presence; they're all past the level of the work we do and they could take whatever admissions test they need in English if they'd just get their confidence screwed up right. Teaching twelve-year-olds fresh from a rural school-less no-where or a war-zone refugee camp is *something*, but this job has been a low-paying coffee break of nothing. I can get more money being a press junket whore and it will leave me with more free time to worry about my health, be homesick, resist liking West Hollywood, and write the kind of stuff I enjoy most, whatever that is.

It also gives me time to watch *King Kong vs. Godzilla* on cable. Morocco plops down on the couch to help me kill a Sunday afternoon doing this.

"Why are they fighting? That's my main plot concern," I

tell Morocco. "It feels inorganic."

"Are you not aware of how Monkey is the historical enemy of Lizard?" asks Morocco.

"Yes," I say. "But it's still a big world. You'd think they'd just stay in their own countries and not stress."

"Monsters don't détente well. Plus there's the issue of them all being rounded up to live on Monster Island. It's a cramped little place."

We watch and learn that King Kong's big secret is that electricity makes him stronger, which helps him deliver the beat-down to Godzilla.

"I really hate this ending," says Morocco. "Godzilla should never not win. I want to see the Japanese version where Kong gets beat."

"Urban legend," I say. "All you get in the Japanese version is the suggestion that Godzilla isn't killed by Kong. They don't mind split-decisions over there."

Then we watch *Godzilla vs. the Smog Monster*, the most psychedelic of the *Gojira* genre, also the most political since it's all about the Ecology, man.

"See, this was back in the day when some serious motherfuckers battled Godzilla," I say. "None of this new shit where he fights fake-ass monsters like Biollante, which is nothing more than a giant bush. Run, everybody. Run from the big flower."

The phone rings. It's Tom Ford. He's going to some industry party at the Abbey for someone's TV show or record release or something stupid like that. The Abbey is a very popular hangout/bar/fashionably gay cruising spot that I've successfully avoided since moving here. And Morocco forgot that he agreed over two weeks ago to go to this party with

Tom, so our cuddly couch time of monster-fighting has to come to an end.

"Come with me," he says.

"To Gay Town?" I ask. "No way."

"You *live* in Gay Town already," he replies. "You're the mayor."

"I'm the janitor. And I must have forgotten to let you know during the first four years of our relationship that, at all times, I am rubber and you are glue. So that means you're the true mayor of Gay Town. Plus, I have this couch here and it needs me. We're in love."

Thirty minutes later Tom Ford rings the doorbell. "What's up, bitches. We ready?" he asks.

"Dave's not going," says Morocco.

"Fucking Dave White. Get your fat ass off that sofa and fucking come with us. You've never been here and I want to see how you react to the Abbey."

My life has come to this point, where I'm the guy that people want to drag to unpleasant destinations so they can watch me become surly and hateful. I'm the Godzilla of my newly-arranged social circle. "So I should come along for your amusement?" I ask.

"I don't know what kind of time you'll have there," says Tom. "But I love how I can never predict how you'll respond to stuff I just take for granted."

I want to prove everyone wrong. I want to make a go of being a West Hollywood Ghetto Gay. At the very least I want to be able to fake it if I have to. So I go.

The Abbey is just a place. It's neither good nor bad. No public space outside of a Wal-Mart or Starbucks is inherently evil. But I have nothing to say to the sea of Little Gay

Shirts that I find myself set adrift on. This Little Gay Shirt is a producer. This other Little Gay Shirt is a makeup artist. The Little Gay Shirts know about cocktails. They talk about the gym. They talk about Britney Spears. And the consensus is that all three are pretty great. But all I can think are horrible thoughts, horrible condescending thoughts that won't make me any friends here, and so I remain silent. Then they walk away. I'm an abject failure at being a normal human being.

"Help me," I say to Morocco.

"We don't have to stay that long," he says.

"No, I mean help me stop being such a critical, judgmental, snooty cockwad," I say. "I have no reason to hate these people but all I want to do is mow them down with some electrical King Kong shit."

"You *are* kind of a homophobe," says Morocco.

"No no no, I'd hate them if they were straight too," I say.

"You're just not trying hard enough," he says. "Make conversation. You're a teacher, pretend you're teaching and win them over. And of the two of us, you're technically the nice one. You're polite and tactful. You can 'yes, and' them all day if you just apply yourself."

"I try the 'yes, and.' And then the conversation just dies on the vine," I say. "I'm really being as bland as I can be here and it's not working."

"Well, I don't know what to tell you," he shrugs.

A fresh Little Gay Shirt approaches us. He knows Tom. I'm introduced as a recent transplant. "And where are you from?" LGS asks me.

"Texas."

"Eww. Too many hicks!" says LGS, shaking his head vigorously.

"I'm a hick," I say.

"Well thank God you got away! Now," he says, straightening himself up like a kindergarten teacher, focusing his eyes intently on me as a weird smirk creeps up from his bowels to his lips, "What do you doooo?" He stretches out the last word to remind me that we can all escape our horrible origins, leave our old selves behind, and become More and Better in This Town if we just apply ourselves.

"I'm a housewife."

"FABULOUS!" says LGS. "I wish I was!"

"I write too."

"Oh?" LGS cocks his brows. "Where have I seen your work?"

"Magazines. Websites. Not TV or movies or anything."

"Oh. I don't read magazines. No time. I produce. Do you have an agent yet?"

"Do I need one?"

"Honey, yes! You'll get nowhere in writing without one!"

"How fast will I go there?"

"What?"

"Nowhere. Can I go there now? Fast?"

"I don't…Oh, I see someone I have to say hello to." He kisses Tom. "Good luck to you, Dan," he says to me. Then he walks away.

We leave the Abbey and Tom Ford drops us off at our place. "You know? I just thought of something," I say.

"What?" asks Morocco.

"I'm not a homophobe. Well not entirely. I think I'm an *industry* phobe. I mean, technically I'm part of the entertainment journalism world now, which I suppose kind of sort of makes me a cog in the wheel, but I hate the idea that it's going to turn me into a wearer of Little Gay Shirts and drinker of cocktails and a bleacher of hair and a not-eater-of-delicious-pies and a person who cares about whether someone's A- or B- or C-list and a person who wants to hang out at the Abbey and talk about getting my screenplay produced and you know…a douche."

"Oh baby…" says Morocco, touching my head tenderly and kissing me gently." Don't worry about that sort of thing. You're already a douche."

Other stuff that happens:

1. Morocco's shiny bald head is not shiny now, it's stubbly. He wears a baseball cap to cover the growing-back-in process. Above the bill, the cap reads, in big red letters: Valley of the Dolls. *I wasn't kidding before.*

2. Vaginal Davis's club Sucker is defunct. Now he's got a new one that he's started up with tattooed, performance-art sexpot Ron Athey. It's called G.I.M.P. I check it out in Silverlake by myself. Morocco Mole falls asleep early that night, maybe intentionally. The main event involves Vag impersonating the Italian artist Vanessa Beecroft and staging a mock-recreation of Beecroft's human installation event where she convinced a squad of Navy Seals to stand at rest in their uniforms while she photographed them and onlookers stared at them all doing that one thing. Vag's crazed, blousy, crooked wig version of this involves repeated shouts of "bellissimo!" and stripping the faux military boys down to their underwear, calling a guy from the crowd of onlookers up to the stage to be a fluffer for his choice of fake cadet, and then directing underground filmmaker Bruce LaBruce to snap pictures of the ensuing blow job while

Vag reads from the United States Military Code of Conduct Handbook. *If I'm diseased with cancer then this can be part of my chemotherapy.*

MASSACRE

WAITING SEVEN ENTIRE days for lump news allows me plenty of time to brood while going about my daily routine. And that routine, sun-shunner that I am, involves moving from the computer screen—where I write short reviews of new CDs and movies—to the TV, where I catch up on the programming aimed at the unemployed, and then back again. I watch "Oprah" with a regularity that alarms Morocco Mole. Today's show is about moms who died of breast cancer and how their kids were sad. I don't need this shit. I flip around the channels. HBO's got *Stepmom,* the one where Susan Sarandon—again with the Susan Sarandon—croaks of cancer at Christmas and leaves her kids homemade quilts. I watch for a while, fantasizing about having my male breast cancer in a really big, expensive house. The phone rings. It's Maryam. "Hey, what are you doing right now?"

"Moping."

"Awesome. Where did you buy your sofa?"

"A store called Shelter," I say. "It's on Beverly."

"I need a new sofa," she says. "Go shopping with me."

We end up sitting on five different couches at Shelter, talking with the wonderfully U.K.-accented Caroline, the woman who helped me and Morocco buy ours. We bought the least expensive one they sold. Maryam's cooing over the pricier ones.

"How are you settling in to West Hollywood?" Caroline asks me.

"Oh, I'm fine," I say. I'm thinking about my lump, not my bottom-feeder writing life, my fear that I'll never make friends as close as the ones I left three states behind, my sense of being constantly overwhelmed by this strange city, the one that I hate just as much as the day the Evil Fuckers wouldn't let us into our apartment, the one that's probably given me cancer.

"You're such a liar!" laughs Maryam. "All he does is complain about every little thing that's happened to him since he got here," she says.

"I believe you've expressed some of your own discontent about this place," I say.

"Yes, but I go out and have fun and meet cute boys in bands," says Maryam. This is true. She prowls the clubs in outfits that make heterosexual men whimper, takes the hearts of beautifully inked rocker dudes, and devours them. When they call her begging for more destruction, she's already moved on to the next hot guy in the newer, buzzier band. She continues, "My only discontent is that I'm not independently wealthy. You have Morocco and so you do your job—your very cool job I have to say—and then you go home to him and bitch about it."

"My job is lame. It's populated by weirdos. My job—"

"Is one lots of people would kill for," she says, capping my sentence with shut-it-whiner finality.

"I'm from London," offers Caroline. "And that's not a small city. But this place *is* serious culture shock. But from what she's saying, Dave, you've voluntarily immersed yourself in a career you don't like."

"I like the writing on the computer all day part," I say. "It's all those other people I can't stand."

The three of us spend the next fifteen minutes commis-erating over our alien status on the very soft sofa. It's covered in a chocolate brown velvet. If it turns out I have cancer I want to come back and lie down on it every day and pretend I'm the Susan Sarandon who gets to live. Maryam wants to look at other options and other stores before buying, but I know she's wrong if she gets anything other than this specific couch with its curative powers.

My next day's afternoon of self-pity is interrupted by work. Fucking work. It's dumb. My task today is to watch a movie that I'm certain is going to eat a dick sandwich, the movie that finally breaks my will to fight. I call Maryam again. "Hey what are you doing right now?"

"I just got home from Barneys. There was this coat there that I really wanted. It was $700 so I had to think about it for a really long time. Then I went and tried it on and didn't buy it and then I went back again and there were only two in my size and then one was gone, and really, do you think $700 is a lot for a coat? I decided to get it. It looks *soooo* good on me."

"I think everyone looks good in $700 coats," I say. "You could have bought seven assy-looking $100 coats and been sad in each one. You made the right decision. Do you want to see a free movie with me?"

"Yeah, when?"

"Three o'clock. Oh yeah, but it's only free for me. Your ticket will cost $700. You can just give me the money and I'll make sure it gets into the right hands."

The screening room is on Sunset. Maryam comes along.

She's wearing the $700 coat, and she's right, it destroys. We get there early because the room is very small and we don't want to be left out. I have to turn in my review the next day and this is the last press screening so I take no chances. Famous film critic Leonard Maltin walks in and sits right next to me. I pretend I don't know who he is and keep talking to Maryam, but she recognizes him too and starts grinning at me like a mental patient. I give her the "be cool" stare. She's not as clear on the concept of not engaging the well-known unless you have specific business with them. And even then, call their publicist first. Maryam and I are talking about movies we've seen, ones we haven't, and ones Morocco's told me I should catch before they leave town. Just then I sense Leonard Maltin turn his head toward us. "Excuse me, but I couldn't help overhearing your conversation. Are you talking about Morocco Mole?" (Note to readers who might be kind of slow: Of *course* Leonard Maltin didn't call him Morocco Mole. But I'm not going to give up his true identity just to make the story more accurate *now*. I've already compressed so many real-life people into composite characters it's not even funny. And you were none the wiser. So just pretend Leonard Maltin really called him his fakey book name. And if you're super-dying to know his real name, just go to the acknowledgments page and guess which person it is.)

It turns out that Morocco knows Leonard Maltin from his old film festival job in Texas, and now through the L.A. Film Critics Association. Funny, he never mentioned to *me* that he was on a "Lenny" basis with Leonard Maltin. It takes Leonard Maltin himself to give me this bit of news. Suddenly, I shift into L.A. blasé about the famous movie critic sitting next to me, and I joke with him like we're pals. I pretend

I've never heard of him before in my life. I pretend we're old drinking buddies. I pretend that next week I'm meeting Ebert for lunch to jovially rib him over how he's so wrong about his dislike of Abbas Kiarostami movies.

The film starts. Over the opening credits music, I sense slight noise and motion coming from my right. I look down to see my new film-critic pal unwrapping some kind of chocolate candy. Right on! I can smell it, I can hear the crinkly paper, I can taste the choco-goodness on my lips. Clearly he's going to share. We're friends now. We both know my domestic partner and agree that he's pretty swell. Obviously this candy is going to seal the deal on our new friendship. He puts a piece in his mouth, chews, swallows, and starts to unwrap a second one.

Then a third.

I'm getting shut out. He eats a few more pieces, greedy bastard, and my watering mouth wants to yell, "Gimme some of that damn candy, Leonard Maltin! Don't you care that I'm DYING of breast cancer?!" Then he's done, like he hasn't betrayed me at all. I spend the remainder of the movie envisioning my doomed lump growing and the doctors saying, "If only he'd enjoyed life more often, stopped to smell the roses, eaten more candy, maybe he'd be alive today."

I mentally write my will while the reels change, leaving everything to Morocco but nothing to that candy-hoarding Leonard Maltin.

Other stuff that happens:
1. I'm sitting on the couch eating Ben & Jerry's Chocolate Fudge Brownie ice cream and watching an autopsy show on cable. I've just returned home from a morning of teaching and then running domes-

tic errands and I'm celebrating my almost-joblessness, not thinking about my freefall into the void of nonstop hustling for freelance writing work. This means more junkets and already I'm having buyer's remorse about my decision. Freelancing would be a lot cooler if it came with guaranteed regular checks. It's the middle of the afternoon. I'm wearing boxer shorts and nothing else because it's already starting to warm up to summer temperatures again. The front door is wide open. Without warning, without so much as the sound of footsteps coming up the stairs to our second-floor perch, the screen door opens and a stranger sticks his head inside. He has dirty blond hair and is wearing dress pants, shirt, and tie. "Anybody home?" he says, grinning.

"Fuck!" I yell, leaping off the couch with a degree of spring and bounce that I didn't know I had in me. "Get the fuck out of my house!"

"Oops, sorry!" he says and backs away. "I didn't mean to frighten you!" He's still grinning.

"Whaddaya want?!"

"I represent blahblahcompany and I'd like to talk to you about blahblah magazine subscriptions and—"

"Is this your first day on the job?!"

"No sir, it's not!" Still with the grinning.

"Then you should fucking know better than to just stick your head into strangers' front doors. Where I come from they shotgun folks like you for trespassing. Now beat it!" I slam the door.

When Morocco comes home from work, the front door is locked and he has to use his key to get in. "Why do you have the door locked?" he asks. I tell him the story.

"I'm sure you scared him more than he scared you," he says.

"Yes, that's what they told the Zodiac Killer's victims after they were murdered," I say.

"How were you dressed?"

"Like I am now," I say. "All sexy. With my sensual belly call-ing out like a siren for him, stoking his insatiable desire to sell us a subscription to Woman's Day. And then possibly to chainsaw massacre me."

"Then you were asking for it."

2. IFILM.com, my main employer, is undergoing changes. What kind I don't know. My editor just got bumped up the ladder and a new one is taking her place. He left me a phone message, asking me to call him back. It would be just my luck that they'd dump me days before I dump the ESL school.

LOATHING

"YOU TOLD ME you were not going to work a short time and then quit," says the Language School's Office Manager.

"Well, I have a new job," I lie. Why do I lie? I wish I knew. In fact, I wish I knew what I was going to tell her next because up to this moment, lying wasn't in my plan. I have nothing more to offer her. "So in a few weeks when this round of courses is finished I will have to leave."

"What is your new job?"

"I'm, um, the new editor-in-chief of a magazine." More lies.

"Oh really? Congratulations. We certainly can't stand in the way of your success. What is the name of the magazine?"

"Honcho."

"I do not know about it."

"It's fashion for men."

It turns out that I have a benign fibrous mass. Muscletissue behaving weirdly and faking me out in a little muscle clump. Or something like that. But no cancer. It happens.

I come home from the doctor with the good news. "Oh good," says Morocco Mole. "I knew you were just being a hypochondriac, as usual."

"Well there *is* a fibrous mass," I argue. "Technically it's almost nearly just like having a real tumor. Of real cancer. I could have died."

"Yes, all of what you say is true. Except totally not," he says from the bathroom, where he's motioning for me to come help rub sunblock into the stubbly scalp. "Best of all, now you'll live to torment Leonard Maltin another day."

"I have a plan, too," I say. "At the next press screening I'm going to sneak in a big plate of Roscoe's chicken and waffles, find where he's sitting, plop myself down right next to him, and then not share."

"Wow, you're almost unbearably diabolical," says Morocco, yawning. "How does the planet absorb all the pure evil you radiate? Could it be that you'll bring about the End Times?"

"I will scorch your bald skull with the fire of my wrath," I say. "No SPF will protect you from this dark retribution. Leonard Maltin will rue the day. He'd better be ready for the Waffle Destruction."

But no Leonard Maltin materializes. It's like he knows.

I focus on dealing with the last few weeks of the English conversation course and with making sure I have enough empty-calorie freelance work to match the stipend-paltry checks that job was producing. Morally questionable pieces about python-skin accessories for spring, junkets for Rob Schneider movies, movie reviews, asking for an *Instinct* raise now that I'm contributing features on gay exploitation films like Redd Foxx's mid-seventies gay-bashing laffer *Norman, Is That You?* and Vietnam-era sissy-fests like *The Gay Deceivers,* and getting my very first music reviewing assignment for the *Advocate.* They need a gay who can write about hip-hop. Hell, they need a gay who *listens* to hip-hop. I'm their gay. My job is to review the latest CD from alleged gay-hater Eminem. So I do, positively, suggesting that Eminem might be smarter than listeners perceive him to be, a creator of characters—something fairly common in hip-hop—whose threats to stab lesbians and gay men in the head are to be taken no more seriously than Britney's plea to hit her one more time, no matter how attractive that prospect might sound. And I receive gay hate mail for my efforts. I'm called self-loathing, ignorant, and traitorous. One review in one magazine and I'm already one of those boring "rebel" journalists.

"Let's go out to dinner to celebrate my cancerlessness and my burgeoning career as a crash-test dummy for the gay media," I say to Morocco Mole.

"Where?"

"Marie Callender's," I say. "I want strawberry pie."

Marie Callender's is where you take a visiting parent, it's where old people go at four o'clock in the afternoon for the senior special, it's where families can all agree to disagree. It's food for people who don't really care that much about food. But they have tongue-spasm-inducing strawberry pie.

"Why didn't we go somewhere else and then come here for just the pie?" asks Morocco, halfway through our filling, bland meal.

"By committing to an entire meal here, I'm reminding myself that I'm part of the mainstream. I enjoy boring entrees and strawberry pies like everyone else. I fit in. I bet Eminem eats here sometimes."

"And I bet Eminem is hanging on every word of this blip in the gay media's coverage of his career, too," says Morocco. "You'll run into him someday and go, 'Yo or whatever, Eminem, my dog! I'm down with your mad skills and dope beats and I, too, enjoy raping bitches and hos and stabbing motherfucking faggots and lezzies in the head and also strawberry pie!' "

"Shhh from the piehole," I say. "This here's a family restaurant. No raping and stabbing talk. Will the *Advocate* want me to write for them some more, do you think? I don't have to fuck shit up every time at bat. I can be gay-friendly too."

"Says you," says Morocco.

From Marie's we wander across the street to the La Brea Tar Pits. It's a month or so past the beginning of daylight saving time, so our post-dessert sun is lingering and making the dirty air a pinky-orange. Weetzie Bat would like this. We breathe in the Wilshire Boulevard exhaust and the toxic fumes from the tar pit. "Imagine if we actually smoked cigarettes too," I say, as we watch the tar pit bubbles gurgle and pop. "We might explode into fireballs right here."

"And you'd like that," adds Morocco.

Other stuff that happens:

1. The Diamanda Galas show, at long last. I take Dave 2, whose first exposure to her singing happens on the night of the concert. In any other circumstance, for any other performer, this would be no big deal. But Diamanda Galas is special. I described her voice to Dave 2, perhaps somewhat deceitfully, as operatic. But the truth is more like…okay, imagine you're watching the movie Halloween, *except that instead of Jamie Lee Curtis running from the masked murderer, it's Maria Callas, and she's screaming for her life and belting out a difficult aria at the same time. That's Diamanda Galas. She can contort her voice into shapes that do not sound like they should come from normal human lungs. To me her voice is a thing of great and terrible beauty. Morocco refuses to join me ("Why would a person pay to hear that in person?" he asks) which spooks me into thinking*

I have to trick Dave 2 into it. But to my surprise, Dave 2 is more than receptive, he's enthusiastic when Miss Galas walks out on stage, sits at the lone black piano and begins the funeral march-like, stalker version of the Supremes' "My World Is Empty without You." Then she sings songs in Italian, Greek, German, French, Spanish, and at least one that's not in any decipherable language. It sort of sounds like a cross between speaking in tongues, ululating, and dry-heaves. She makes it work.

Then there's the matter of the audience. There are post-goth thirtysomethings like me and Dave 2, in various shades of gray and black. There's the man in the FUCK JESUS T-shirt ("What did Jesus ever do to that guy?" asks Dave 2). There's the tranny dude in the drum majorette/Nazi SS officer/Wendy & Lisa gear with the sparkly ankh earrings. There's the woman wrapped in Clan of the Cave Bear *animal pelts, a large black stripe of eye makeup on her face and a big fake rhinoceros horn affixed to her forehead. But none are as shocking as the people seated a few rows ahead of us. They're a group of three, and after the fourth song, the person seated in the middle of the threesome announces, loudly, "Daddy, I wanna get out of here!" and begins to cry. There's a world of difference between being a cool parent and being a smart one.*

2. Celebrity sighting: Holly Hunter and her Spielberg cinematographer husband Janusz Kaminski. They're in line in front of me at Pavilions supermarket. She's reading the Enquirer. *They have a lot of store brands in their basket, which makes me like them more than I have any reason to. When you come up hardscrabble in the American South or Eastern Europe, you don't piss away your money.*

WORTHLESS

"WILL YOU GET another bag of gorgeous free items from this one?" asks Morocco Mole.

"I better," I say. "I need some worthless shit to sell in a future garage sale."

I'm going to another junket today. An "indie" movie. Except it's produced by Danny DeVito and stars Kevin Spacey, who's won something like nine Oscars already, so it's really more like IndieWood. The closest thing to a no-name indie actor in it is some dude from *Can't Hardly Wait* named Peter Facinelli.

"Where's it at?" he asks me.

"Planet of the Apes–Land."

"Well, have a good time. Conquest them. If you get the chance, be sure to give Kevin Spacey the rundown."

But the award-winning actor is nowhere to be found in this Century City hotel. We get the director. We get the young Facinelli fellow. We get Danny DeVito. But we get no Big Guy. He's too busy to promote this small movie he's in. He's got better things to do than sit in a room full of dumbshits with tape players who might ask him inappropriate personal questions. But up until we discover he's a no-show, we, the junket press, are led to believe by the publicists that he may very well make an appearance. We're giddy and happy to know that he *might* show. We sit and eat the buffet food and speculate on whether or not we'll get Spacey. That will make the day. It'll give us something to bring home to our editors. And eventually we get to that sick collective point where we're actually longing for him. He's the prom date who said he'd be here at 8:00 but now it's 8:30 and we're thinking maybe he's just running late and then it's 9:00 and we're thinking maybe he's had an accident and we worry about his well-being and then it's 10:00 and we're getting angry because, you know what, he could have called, it's not like phones aren't everywhere, and by 10:30 we're eating a pint of ice cream on the couch, saying, "Fuggit." One of the junketeers begins packing up his tape player and walks out. DeVito, however, very nearly makes up for it all by bouncing into the room and being raucously funny and talking shit about Spacey in his absence. Affectionate shit, which is not the kind of shit we'd like to hear most right now, but all the same he helps make us all the teeniest bit less pissed off about wasting a day in the hope of chasing down the elusive movie star. And about the miniscule amount of swag-bribery. Fucking indie films.

But really, why *did* I just sit through half a day of doing nothing for so little? Oh yeah, it's because this is what I do with my life now. Because I suck. I suck for having this big idea that I'm going to write for a living, I suck for not getting with the program and loving my status as a hack, bottom-slurping entertainment "journalist," and most of all for not dressing better for the occasion in order to distance myself from the rest of the disheveled bunch. (My own brother, a heterosexual lawyer into body-building and well-tailored suits, calls me and Morocco "a pair of unmade beds.")

"Well at least you showed up," says Morocco later that night as he listens to me complain. "That means you suck less than Spacey."

But privately we both know that's not a small enough amount of suck.

Other stuff that happens:

1. My mom is coming to visit. No reason, she's just coming. We need a place for her to sleep. We decide to invest in a new mattress for us and move our old one into the apartment's second bedroom as a guest bed. And in West Hollywood, where a person might mistakenly believe he or she would find a queer-operated mattress store, where a person goes to buy what is, at least for part of his or her horizontal life, a sex cushion, there is no such thing. So we head off to one in Culver City that's having a sale.

When we enter the store, there are two middle-aged guys hanging around doing nothing. Morocco and I move from firm to soft to firm again, touching each mattress delicately, hands only.

"Who needs the mattress?" says the salesman whose nametag reads "Bill."

"Us," I say, because, you know, fuck this sudden senseless intimidation. "We need something firm and sturdy. We're not small."

"Well, go ahead and get on it. Try it out," says Bill.

Morocco and I hop on the bed and lie down next to each other. Back in Texas, we were more than once perceived to be brothers, to which I'd always say, "No, boyfriends," giving them my surliest demeanor, daring them to start shit. They had no idea I was the biggest pussy of all time and had never ever been in anything even remotely resembling an actual fistfight, but I can serve face and mass and it usually works. It's at this moment I realize that Bill just wants our money. Two fat faggots? This bed will absolutely hold 500 pounds of gay sex! Simulate anal if you want, just drop that thousand bucks.

So we do. Drop the thousand bucks, that is.

2. Things to do while standing in line waiting to check in at the press table at a local multiplex so you can see a big-budget piece of shit and then review it but dang you forgot to bring a book to read (do them in order or it's no good):

Stare at Winona Ryder as she stands in the theater lobby, talking into a cell phone and looking at a poster for a movie she's not even in. Admire her black trench coat but wonder why she's got it on in this spring weather that's not even a little bit cold. Wonder what designer it is. Think about how it would be funny if you just went over and snapped her phone shut in mid-conversation, standing between her and the poster she is trying to look at, blocking her view, and how you'd say, "Girl, you're interrupted." It would at least be funny to you.

Stop staring when she looks in your direction.

Recognize another actor in the lobby, this time female and African-American, a character actor who plays lots of judges on law shows and whose name you can't remember or never knew. Maybe she hangs out at Silver Spoon too.

Get asked by random strangers—strangers who already bought a ticket to something else so why they care baffles you—what movie you're standing in line to see. Answer truthfully the first three times.

On the fourth time say, "The Swarm. *It's about these killer bees that come to America and sting everyone to death."*

"The Day the Clown Cried. *I hear it's supposed to be like* Life Is Beautiful. *I guess we'll see, won't we?"*

"Goin' Coconuts. *It's a comedy set in Hawaii. Computer-generated monkeys, too, like in* Jumanji."

Listen to the woman behind you begin to say made-up shit too. Hear her go so far as to say that you're both in line for an exclusive sneak preview of a movie that's a secret and that even our presence in line is an exclusive secret and that we got on the invite list because of powerful people we know.

Watch three Japanese people stare intently at your Princess Mononoke T-shirt like they're either a) all jealous of your incredible T-shirt style or b) thinking you're the White Devil.

I play phone tag with my new IFILM editor, but from what I can understand from his messages, I have to come down to his office to meet him to discuss my future.

CORPSE

JUNE IS MY birthday month, so naturally I've been thinking about death. The truth, though, is that I like to think about dying for a little bit each day. It comforts me. I consider my options, like how old I'll be when I go, what disease will take root in my geriatric body, and what my legacy will be to future generations. I mentally design my headstone. Morocco Mole wants to be cremated and then have his ashes flung off some cliff or something, which I feel is a waste of a good funeral. I want to be buried in the ground in a smart suit and I want my friends to make some casseroles. It should be on a blustery, forty-degree November day, overcast and threatening to rain. I'll have gone after gathering everyone I know around my bed and saying my last farewell to Morocco, who'll have my blessing to go out and find someone half as good as I've been. It will prove problematic for him since he'll be about ninety-seven but he's still welcome to go for it.

In a related thread of morbidity, I've also become mildly obsessed with the idea of finding a dead body in the dumpster that's located in the parking garage underneath our apartment building. It could happen. That guy got held-up at gunpoint on the sidewalk across the street not long ago and had he actually been murdered could have ended up tossed in with our empty cereal and pizza boxes. I'd lift the lid, see the decaying corpse, and whisper something like, "Oh my

God." Then I'd change into something stylish and end up interviewed, visibly shaken, on the evening news: "Yes, it was me. I found the body. So shocking. Nothing like this has ever happened in our neighborhood. You think you're safe…."

So while most gays cringe at the thought of growing older, I welcome it. I especially welcome it because it comes with presents and meals out. In fact, I enjoy the entire month of June that way, encouraging everyone I know to fete me. Or at least I did in Texas. Here I'm not so sure what's going to happen. It could be me and Morocco. It could be a love-in, featuring all my new friends. Morocco had better have told them to stand and deliver.

On the Friday night before my birthday, I encourage Morocco Mole to begin the me-celebration at our favorite local diner, Eat Well. It's Fish-n-Chips Special night. As we walk in we notice it's also Horrible Music night. Billy Joel's "We Didn't Start the Fire" is blasting out of the speakers. Whatever. It's not going to soil my golden, battered mercury-cod. Then comes Stevie Wonder and Paul McCartney's "Ebony and Ivory." A watershed moment for both artists, it signaled each one's demise as an entertainer. From that song till now, Stevie Wonder hasn't made a single good record. As for Paul, his greatest pop achievement in almost thirty years has been Stella. Morocco Mole notes, "This must be the *Hits of the Eighties* CD that *Entertainment Weekly* sends you when your subscription check bounces."

The fish and chips arrive, and as I devour the deep-fried meal, Morocco asks what I want to do for my thirty-sixth. First, I share the dumpster/corpse fantasy with him. That would be the start—or finish, I'm not picky—of a perfectly memorable birthday.

"That's nice," he says. "Would you like me to make you an anthrax birthday cake, too? Maybe toast the day with a champagne flute of Liquid-Plumr?"

"I want to find decent barbecue," I say, which isn't the full truth. The full truth is that I want the decent barbecue to find me. I want to be lounging nude on my bed watching *Sleepaway Camp* on Cinemax. (And really, what an awesome movie. Everybody dies and then you find out the killer girl is this teen tranny with a weird little Vienna sausage penis and when you see her in the last scene she's covered in blood and grinning like a mental case—which she is, being the camp serial killer and all—and her penis is just sticking out like it's almost erect. Incredible.) And I want the barbecue ribs to float into the bedroom and hover over my head as the tender meat falls from the bone and into my open mouth. Then Dan Haggerty circa 1979 comes in and licks the barbecue sauce from my chin. Some sweet day this will come true for me. "Other than that," I say, "I have no special desires. I'm expecting my so-called L.A. friends to come over and carry me around on their shoulders, taking me from one excitement to the next."

Lucky me, they do. Friends Dave 2, *Glue* Laurie, Our Tom Ford, Maryam, Sean, Vinny, and Spiritual Andy show up outside our door the next morning. Dave 2 is holding a scuffed, bent photo of a strange woman wearing a halter top, eyes half closed. "Here's your gift," he says. "I found it on the sidewalk. Let's go to the El Capitan to see *Swiss Family Robinson.*"

So we do. It's one of my favorite old Disney films that, in the light of the new century, is offensively racist and sexist, but, still, they fight pirates with coconut bombs and all the animals wear little outfits so, you know, it's pretty great. It's also nice to see that it's even playing at Disney's big-screen outpost on Hollywood Boulevard and that they aren't trying to completely obliterate the idea of the Robinsons from our imagineer-mangled imaginations. They've already remodeled and re-"branded" the Disneyland attraction formerly known the Swiss Family Treehouse. Now it's the Tarzan Treehouse and when you go there they've stationed an orange-tanned actor in a matted Tarzan wig and loincloth outside, beckoning you to enter his lair. The music inside the house has been "upgraded" from the "Swisskapolka" to Phil Collins, his barfy film score creeping into your ears and every pore of your skin like a staph infection.

After the Robinsons, it's time for barbecue. Now, you'd think that West Hollywood, home to carnivorous carbophobes, would feature one good rib joint. It doesn't. In fact, Los Angeles itself is sadly bereft of the sort of barbecue that lives on every street corner in Texas. I've been to not one, but two, places called Real Texas Bar-B-Q in this city, and both of them weren't even good enough to cut it in Oklahoma. That's when Dave 2 and his barbecue sauce–catching beard steps in and whisks us off to the Valley for a visit to Dr. Hogly Wogly's Tyler Texas Bar-B-Que, a name which gives me pause. If you've got the *cojones* to call yourself something like that when fucking palm trees are planted right outside your door, you'd better bring it. I have relatives in Tyler. Those people don't fuck around. But I'm happy to report that Dr. Hogly Wogly's Tyler Texas Bar-B-Que is full-on delicious, my lips, fingers and chin smacking with sauce. Dan Haggerty doesn't show, but I'm showered with love and presents by my new friends and Morocco Mole (CDs by Beat Happening and Nico, a vintage Rock'em Sock'em Robots game) and loving my life for the first time since moving here. And as we exit the restaurant, we pass a dumpster. I peek inside and find nothing but stinky trash.

Other stuff that happens:

1. I clean the apartment for my mother's arrival. Why I do this I don't know. It's not like I grew up in a clean house. We had cats. We had dogs. My mother smoked. My stepfather smoked. All their friends smoked. Our extended family of aunts, uncles, and cousins smoked. I used to keep my bedroom door shut tight year-round and my windows cracked, a Glade Air-Wick full-tilt open at all times and a can of Lysol on my dresser just to ward off the constant creeping atmosphere of saloon. I'd hustle my clothes straight from the dryer and into my bedroom closet to keep them as free of the scent of stale ashtray as possible.

2. I'm sitting in the office of Lew, my new editor at IFILM, and he's telling me that things are about to change. They're changing the way they review movies. Do I want to keep reviewing movies for them? When I tell him that I do, he tells me that they're changing their format to a more fun, readable, entertaining "bullet point" style of film review. No more exhausting prose. From now on it's going to be snappy little categories that will answer questions like, "Is it a date movie?" and, "When is a good time during the movie to take a bathroom break?"

I express enthusiasm to continue working and receiving checks, so now it's my job to turn in samples of this peppy new format. I'm being invited to audition to keep my job.

DECAYING

"GOOD *God,* YOU'RE just like your father," snorts my mother.

I've just picked her up from the airport. I've got a Nancy Griffith CD playing in the car and until this moment I had forgotten her distaste for country music. For thirty-five consecutive years, she endured two alcoholic, job-losing, mortgage-foreclosure-inducing husbands who refused to listen to anything but Johnny Cash and Waylon Jennings, and aside from the occasional Crystal Gayle song my mother will be happy if she never hears another steel guitar again.

What she doesn't understand, though, is that, for me, listening to Nancy Griffith is something of a minor-league victory over homesickness. It's not simply that the woman's songs are Texas-centric, they're also some of the most beer-crying country songs I've ever heard. You think Judas Priest causes suicides? You haven't heard Nancy yodel and wail about some long lost love she left behind in Temple, Texas. If you're melancholy by nature I can't recommend her. I put a song of hers on a tape for Morocco Mole once and he curses me to this day because every time he hears it he tears up.

"I thought you liked all that ugly punky music," continues my mother. She's wearing a cornflower-blue T-shirt that reads "GENUINE ANTIQUE PERSON" and pulling a small ladylike cigar out of a Kate Spade bag. She's taken up smoking again but switched from cigarettes to cigars. It's more feminine.

"You're not doing that in my car," I say.

"I'll blow the smoke out the window," she says.

"Okay, here are the rules," I continue. "All hideous smoking is to take place outside of my car and my house. That's it. No discussion. I'll drop your ass at a hotel. And when did you start smoking cigars? When did you become such a dude?"

"Hush your mouth, now. I like them. You don't have to smoke them," she says.

For the next week, our routine consists of the following: Morocco goes off to work, I deal with whatever work deadlines I have while my mother sits on the apartment balcony, smoking tiny woman-cigars and reading the thousand-page historical romance novel she's brought with her. The afternoons are for tourism. I take her up to Mulholland Drive so she can get a view of our side of the hill as well as the Valley. She's repulsed by the hazy brown air. "Don't complain to me about cigars," she says. "You breathe *that.*"

I take her to Hollywood Boulevard to Grauman's Chinese Theater. In front of the Chinese theater are those footprints in the cement. But that's not why I like taking out-of-towners. I'm a fan of the movie characters, or rather, the unemployed actors who make their living standing outside the theater dressed as famous movie characters and posing for photos with tourists for five bucks a pop. There's Spiderman, Batman, Darth Vader and Darth Maul, Crocodile Dundee, Yoda, Frankenstein, Zorro, and Marilyn Monroe. All of them are lurid specimens, but my favorite is the tall, lanky, greasy-haired, pot-bellied Superman. He stands in the picture with the visibly-shaken tourists, grinning broadly while they force smiles as quickly as possible. They usually see him from across the street, yell, "Hey Superman!" and run up to get their snapshot, only to get a good look—and smell—the closer they get. Watching people recoil from body odor is fun. If he'd only called Pink Dot grocery delivery before clocking in, they would've sent some shampoo and soap to the Fortress of Solitude. "They're all disgusting," says my mother, taking a picture of Frankenstein. "Why do you like them so much?"

"For the same reason you're snapping pictures, maybe? Their shit is fascinatingly broke-down," I say.

"Stop that. You know I don't like profanity."

"Anyway," I continue, "you know how plants lean into the sun? Well, I lean into failure. I know it will always be there for me."

We walk down the block past the Scientology building and its flabbergastingly beautiful vintage neon sign. I mention that Morocco Mole won't allow me to go inside the building to take their "personality test," and my mother says, "Why not? It's no worse than where you came from." And she's right. We're from a state where the Baptist churches have been known to sponsor outreach programs to Jews, hoping to win them to Christ. Texas and Los Angeles are not that far apart in regard to unconventional religiosity.

We walk down to Musso & Frank, the oldest restaurant in Hollywood. It's been around since 1919, is dark and cool inside, and the ancient menu continues to offer items like tongue sandwiches, flannel cakes, and fruit compotes. It's the kind of place you could imagine old-fashioned mobsters planning a hit. We have the flannel cakes and sink ourselves deep into the blood-red banquette. "Where's the smoking section?" asks my mother.

"There isn't one," I explain. "There's no smoking in California bars and restaurants, period. It's the new law and it's one of the reasons, in spite of all the other strikes against it, that I'm going to keep living here."

"I'll be right back then," she says, heading for the back alley exit door, stopping by the kitchen to bum a light from a busboy.

The next day we drive to Santa Monica to wander the Third Street Promenade. We go to the pier to look out at the Pacific Ocean, then head back in to shop. My mother loves to look for cheap jewelry made of rocks and crystals and there are more than a few places here to suit her needs. One of them has a large window display of hand-blown glass bongs. The store carries a huge selection of swirling, psychedelic designs. "Oh! David!" she says excitedly. "Look what they have here!"

"Yes, My Lady Smokesalot? You've taken up reefer along with the Dutch Master Petites? You wanna borrow my Cypress Hill CDs too?"

"Hush now. I don't even know what that Cyber Hill is. And I don't smoke marijuana, silly. I just think that the glass is pretty."

"They're BONGS, Ma. Do you know what a bong is?"

"*Yes,* I know what a bong is. I know they're bongs."

"Admit that you thought it was just a funny vase."

"No," she says. "Stop it. Stop making fun of me. I'm your mother and I've been around bongs."

"Name one time," I say.

"Your cousin," she snaps, and I remember that she's totally

right about that. He used to be a big stoner. Then he went to prison. Forgery. "And you've become awfully belligerent since you moved here."

She's totally right about that, too.

On her final night in town, she's game for a late-night show of *The Poseidon Adventure* at the ancient, decaying Orpheum Theatre downtown. It's a fundraising screening to help the ongoing restoration and they're going to need every cent they get to make this formerly awe-inspiring movie palace feel like a place anyone would want to sit in again. Morocco joins us, and when we walk inside he says, *"The Poseidon Adventure* was a good choice because this place is Hell right-side up."

As it is, I'm afraid rats are going to nibble on my ankles while we watch the movie, so it's my devotion to this, my all-time favorite film, that keeps me from turning around and bolting. But I've got my Ernest Borgnine costume on—a stretched-out, chest-baring, v-neck T-shirt—and I'm ready for the moment when I get to turn to Morocco and say, "You took from me the only thing I ever loved in the whole world! My Linda! You killed her!"

When the tidal wave hits the SS *Poseidon,* Morocco and I take turns flicking bottled water at each other, trying to make sure we both feel the terror of the crashing wave. It's our Sensurround.

Other stuff that happens:

1. Feeling lucky and Poseidonish, *I take my mother to Silver Spoon for her last meal before leaving town, but all we get is Sally Kirkland. She's there every day.*

2. On our way to the airport, I detour us onto Robertson so my mother can enjoy the Kate Spade store. She's flipping out that there's an entire store devoted to her favorite purse-manufacturer and buys a tiny pink clutch. She'll most likely carry cigars in it, but whatever.

3. Celebrity sighting: John Cusack at LAX. I like to imagine the flight attendants constantly having to say, "Pardon?" to everything he says.

REVENGE

THERE'S A REASON I stayed relatively boyfriendless and even gay-friendless until my thirties. That reason is—Morocco Mole is right—I'm a touch misanthropic with regard to a few very specific types of my own gay kind: the politically conservative Caucasian ones who hate that the other freaks who also happen to be homo get in the way of their obvious, God-given right as white men to rule the world; the bears who say "woof" all the time (exception: if I've had a few beers and they're saying it to me); the ones eating broccoli and chicken breasts for breakfast at Eat Well; the ones who tweezer and reshape their eyebrows; the ones who get in my way.

The gays who get in my way 'round these parts bulldoze the streets in their earth-raping SUVs that bleed horrible music. They're invariably Dress-All-Stupid Queens blabbing, "Hey Girl! Yeah, I'm driving! It's *crazy!*" on their cell phones, and then, not content to keep their awfulness to themselves, they try to run me over and decimate me. It's already happened three times in the eleven months I've lived here. The first two—just for recap's sake—were garden-variety near-death experiences delivered by people who couldn't be bothered to notice that driving drunkenly on the sidewalk was against the law. The third one was administered by Oscar-winner Linda Hunt. And I'm now convinced that this new one, my fourth, was deliberate. It's 7:15 A.M. on a Tuesday as I walk back from the supermarket with Pop Tarts—a part of my good breakfast—that I choose to begin eating fresh from their Brown Sugar Cinnamon box as I stroll leisurely across the street, when the light changes. In this neighborhood that's civil disobedience. That's when the carb police officer in his white Escalade decides that he's had enough of my tasty crimes against abs and aims his tank at me. Never mind that he has a red light and I have the pedestrian right-of-way. He wants me dead. As he careens past, he yells out his open window, gross yellow-tinted sunglasses on his orange face, "(GARBLE GARBLE) YOU FAT FUCK!" I'm too busy leaping out of his way to yell my soon-to-be-trademarked-catchphrase of "Eat shit, faggot!" but for half a second I consider throwing the box of Pop Tarts at him. I don't, of course. That'd be cutting off my tongue to spite my ears.

"You really should live in the Valley," says Dave 2. Dave 2 lives in Sherman Oaks, and, as I've mentioned before, is the Beariest Bear in Bear Town. He believes that we should band together and be neighbors. "You're the wrong kind of fag for West Hollywood."

"No, I'm not. *They* are. Plus, it's surface-of-the-sun-hot over there. I don't know how you stand it. It's like sixty degrees cooler on my side of the hill," I protest.

"Well they have these inventions that just came out. Air conditioners. You turn them on and they make the air in your house cool. Also? We have fun stuff to do there. With parking spaces. Plus more lanes on the roads. You're safer."

"Like what fun stuff exactly? Dropping dead from the heat when you step outside your house? Shopping at Wal-

Mart? You people couldn't even save your own historical landmarks."

"What historical landmarks?"

"I'm only speaking of the Sherman Oaks Galleria, of course. So much beautiful mall. So much cultural history. Gutted. Where will future generations go when they want to see the set of *Fast Times at Ridgemont High* or *Chopping Mall?* Where?

"I think I hear a lonely chopping mall in Texas calling your name, my friend."

To soothe me, he points me in the vague direction of the Brady Bunch house that lurks somewhere in Studio City, on his side of the hill. So they haven't destroyed all the historical landmarks, after all. But fat chance trying to find it on your own. You need a guide. A real Valley girl. Or boy. "I'd go with you but I have a lunch date," says Dave 2.

"Is this a B.Y.O.Lube lunch date?" I ask.

"No, really," he says, "I'm serious. Move back to Texas. Now."

I set off in search of the Brady home, and in short order get completely lost. Car horns in my rear-view are blasting for my little un-air-conditioned piece of shit to move dammit and it feels like every molecule of me is melting because I'm trapped in the blistering Valley heat and even if I could find the place it doesn't look the same anymore because obsessives like me have been hounding the poor dumbasses who bought the Tiki-idol-cursed property for like thirty years. You really do need a Valley person to successfully find the Bradys. Or someone else who is not you in your crappy, slow-moving car, who is not sweating profusely like you and who is not holding up traffic like you and who doesn't give up easily like you. You need to stop for a second and pull over and re-collect your thoughts and keep trying. You need to remember that everyone isn't the yellow-sunglasses guy in the white Escalade even if they *are* honking at you. They're honking at you because you're being a moron. You need to understand that sticking it out will more likely get you what you want, even if what you want is something idiotic. But as you drive back home, defeated, headachy, and frazzled, you comfort yourself that at least you've seen Jayne Mansfield's house. Several times.

A cold shower and two Tylenol later, I'm ready for work. I have a press screening to go to. I'm looking forward to it because the private screening rooms are always refrigerated just the way I like them to be. I have to bring a sweatshirt with me even when it's eighty-five degrees outside. In the screening room parking lot under the building sits a steroidal white Escalade but I think nothing of it. Lots of assholes around here drive big white Escalades. They're not just for rappers anymore. It's taking up two spaces in this square-footage-deprived mini-lot because, you know, why not? People with giant tank-ass cars are entitled to all the square-footage they need.

But then, when I step inside, a familiar-faced publicist is there checking names off the list. His Hepatitis-A shades give him away. It's my would-be executioner. Of *course* he's a publicist. It all makes sense now. A buff, gay twentysomething trust-fund kid with an Escalade and poor fashion sense and a studio job he'll leave in two years when he becomes an oily development exec. He has no idea who I am when I walk up and give my name, has no idea I was the Fat Fuck he could have decimated in a clean-break hit-and-run if he'd wanted to. To him I'm just another annoyance. He checks me off the list and I walk inside the screening room. Leonard Maltin is there, sitting on the opposite side. He nods in my direction. I've neglected to bring revenge food.

I drop my bag in my seat and go back outside, downstairs, to my car, ostensibly to look for something. At least as I pass the publicist I silently try to give off the idea that I have innocuous business in the parking lot. But what I'm really looking for is security cameras. Finding none, I approach my target on the side opposite the entrance. If someone happens to drive in while I exact justice, I want to remain relatively hidden. No cars approaching, I make my move.

And then I stop. I have the keys in my hand and inside I'm feeling the bliss of what it would be like if they went gliding and scraping across the length of his paint job. Hepatitis-Man: 0. Fat Fuck: 1. I came down here to do it. I should do it. He deserves to have his awful property vandalized. It would be justice. I'm punk rock. I have a punk-rock duty to smash the state. I didn't stare down the faggot insanity at the theater that other night. I was awestruck by evil then. This is my chance for redemption. I could strike a blow for decency. I could.

Other stuff that happens:

1. Glue Laurie calls me and asks me if I know who Brittany Murphy is. Of course I do. She's the rotisserie chicken suicide chick from Girl, Interrupted and the loony juvey lezzie from Freeway. Clueless too. She's the next Glue cover girl and I'm her interviewer. Time to catch up on her movies.

2. I turn in my three "audition" reviews to Lew. I assume I'll be passed over for someone else and begin scanning the back of a local gay newspaper where guys advertise "personal services" in the back.

All of them have washboard abs. I wonder if there's a belly-fetish niche market I could exploit for a few extra bucks. I'd only need one "client" a day to make up for the amount of money that reviewing movies brings in. Furthermore, it would make an awesome basis for a future "I Was a Chubby Sex Worker" memoir. When I tell Morocco Mole about my genius new prostitution idea, he tells me it will never work. "You don't know how to make change for a five."

3. *It turns out that Linda Ronstadt once shot an album cover photo at Irv's Burgers.*

Sonia tells me that Jimi Hendrix and Janis Joplin also hung out there before they died. Then she says, "You tell the movie actress you interview to come here and eat a burger! She'll become more famous like them!"

5

ACCEPTANCE

ASSAULT

IT'S MY ANNIVERSARY. For the past twelve months in West Hollywood I've lived and died more times than Jason Voorhes. Morocco and I have occupied our too-good-for-us apartment with its decently large floor plan, multiple big windows, long outside balcony, wood floors, fifties-era kitchen tile, and rent control for nearly fifty-one weeks, and it would have been fifty-two had it been vacated when it was time by the Evil Fuckers who lived here before—the ones who refused to budge, who forced the heavenly sister act of Laura and Betty to take pity on us and let us occupy their guest room for nine days, the ones whose smoking made nicotine seep from the bathroom walls for a full six months afterward, the ones who didn't even bother to leave address-forwarding notices with the post office and whose mail, including all their tax forms, still gets delivered here. We just laugh and throw it away. "Ha, ha," we say, as we toss.

And I no longer feel overwhelming fear and disdain for my new home. Twelve months beats a person down. I don't have the energy to engage in 24/7 place-hate, even if I'm still frequently bewildered by its ways. I don't understand wearing flip-flops everywhere, every day, no matter the weather. I don't understand coupling them with a knit cap or scarf. I don't understand heterosexual men who tint their eyelashes. I don't understand why I don't get a say in whose picture winds up on the gigantic, building-sized Gap ad that's permanently affixed to the side of a tall building on Sunset, a building I can see clearly every day from my kitchen window. I don't understand why anyone would live in the far reaches of the valleys where summer means fires that annually engulf dozens of homes. I don't understand buying a home in the Hollywood Hills either, with its threat of mudslides every time it rains for more than two days in a row. I don't understand the disproportionate numbers of people here who believe that they, not the sun, are the center of it all. And most of all I don't understand why more of the other folks don't call them on their fucked up bullshit.

I'm at the Sunset 5, a movie theater that's a block and a half from our apartment. It's attached to the Virgin Megastore on Sunset Boulevard. I drove there. Remember at the beginning of this story where I wrote about how lucky I felt to be in a neighborhood where I could walk to the things I needed? Well, fuck that. I was stupid then. I drive everywhere now. I've had enough of other bitches and their cars trying to take me out. From now on if you crash into me then I'm going to crash you back.

I'm here to watch *Trixie,* an Alan Rudolph movie starring Emily Watson, Nathan Lane, Nick Nolte, and Brittany Murphy. It turns my brain to oatmeal. My interview subject's performance, however, is entertainingly loopy. She is, in fact, the only part of the movie I can stand. I'll just avoid it as a topic of conversation. If she agrees not to bring it up, then I'll agree too.

I take the elevator down to my car, drive back up to the exit level, and encounter a short line at the parking attendant's box. There seems to be a problem with the car stalled outside

the box. It's a small four-door, it's filled with Hispanic teenagers, and it's not moving. It appears that they've lost their
parking ticket and don't have the automatic ten-dollar fee
charged to all vehicles with lost tickets. I'm third in line. In
my rear-view mirror I see more cars coming to a halt and the
line grows. The teenage girl working in the ticket booth is ar-
guing with the teenagers in the car. She refuses to lift the gate
for them until they find the ten dollars. Horns begin honking. A man on foot passes my window. He's walking toward
the booth. Then he shouts, as menacingly as his Gay Voice
will allow him to, "What the FUCK is the problem here?"

The Hispanic teenagers seem startled by the angry homo.
They want no trouble and roll up their windows.

Teen Girl in Ticket Booth: "Mumble mumble something." She waves her hand in the direction of the ticketless
and moneyless car.

Gay Voice: "Open this fucking gate NOW!"

Teen Girl in Ticket Booth: "Sir, I can't mumble mumble
something."

Gay Voice: "I don't give a fuck about your rules! I have to
leave! I have somewhere to go! All these other people have
to leave too! Open this fucking gate!"

Teen Girl in Ticket Booth is just trying to do the right
thing in a difficult situation. She most likely makes minimum
wage. It's fairly certain she'll be reprimanded, or worse, if
she lets ticket-non-havers through without paying. But Gay
Voice has all the markings of an Entitlement Queen: blond,
muscular, and tan, clearly having just finished his workout at
Crunch. In my rear-view mirror I see that he's left open the
door to his white Escalade.

And when he turns, his unmistakable profile is that of the

Hepatitis Sunglasses–wearing, Fat Fuck–flattening publicist whose SUV I failed to key in revenge because I'm pathetic and spineless. And why is he turning? Because he's entering the ticket booth. It's his duty to force Teen Girl to open the gate. She tries to block his entry and he pushes her aside, grabs her arm, and attempts to hit the right button. She's crying and shouting. I sit and watch, briefly stunned.

Just then, the man in the car between the Hispanic teenagers and me leaps out of his driver's side door. He's big and mean-looking, like an ex-con who's trying really hard to fit back into society, praying to the Lord each day for the strength not to violate his parole. He barks, "Buddy, you better fuckin' relax and get back to your fuckin' car!"

But Gay Voice Hepatitis Shades Publicist is undeterred. He's scuffling with Teen Girl, who's now crying uncontrollably and trying to break free from Gay Voice's grip. That's when Ex-Con guy takes a few menacing steps toward the booth and repeats himself. "NOW!" he bellows.

This time Gay Voice gets the message, lets go of Teen Girl, and slinks back to the Escalade, making sure to steer clear of Ex-Con, who by this point is standing with outstretched arms in that pose that's the universal symbol for, "You wanna go? Let's do it here and I'll fuck your shit *up.*"

Teen Girl hits the gate-lift button. The Hispanic teenagers leave black marks on the concrete—they can't get out of there fast enough. Ex-Con returns to his car and, apparently secure in the knowledge that he'd done his good deed for the day, drives off, too.

I drive up to the box. "He assaulted you. Are you hurt?"

Teen Girl can't speak because she's still crying hysterically.

"Did you call security?" I ask.

"Yes," she manages between sobs. She grabs my ticket and pushes the button to let me out. I drive past the gate and pull over to the side of the exit. Another car exits as I get out. Now it's the Escalade's turn to leave. Gay Voice hands Teen Girl his ticket like they've never met before. His face is sociopath calm. I walk up to his grill and stand in front of the Escalade, not sure what I'll do if he gets out again, but at least for now, I plan to dare him to run me over. Fortunately I don't have to think about a plan for very long. Two security guards are running up to the box. I say, "Him. That guy. He did it. He assaulted her."

Gay Voice Publicist gets out of the Escalade again, scowling and screaming, "What the fuck did you see? What the fuck are you talking about? You didn't see shit!"

"Shut up, bitch!" I can't believe how loudly I'm yelling, but I am. "I SAW YOU GRAB THAT GIRL'S ARM AND HURT HER! I SAW YOU ASSAULT HER! I SAW EVERYTHING!" Suddenly I feel very Batman. Or at least very *Get Christie Love.*

Gay Voice Hepatitis Shades Publicist is handcuffed and taken away. One of the security guys takes my statement before leading me back to the holding area. I can only imagine the number of Virgin Megastore shoplifters who've passed through this room. I'm asked to wait outside a few moments, then I'm led in, just as Gay Voice is being *uncuffed* and *released.* It turns out that he's apologized to Teen Girl, who, still trying to catch her breath and stop sobbing, has agreed not to press charges. Gay Voice is ushered out past me, not looking in my direction, and not about to get the inconvenient several-hour stay in the pokey he deserves, so I offer him a little L.A. advice, "Get some therapy, asshole."

Other stuff that happens:

1. *My fears of losing my IFILM movie-reviewing job have proven unfounded. I get to keep doing it. In fact, I get to keep doing it a lot. What I didn't quite understand—maybe I wasn't paying attention, which is totally possible—was that they were looking to get rid of all their film critics. Except one. And I'm going to be the one. According to Lew, I'll have my own weekly column that I can use to bitch about sucky movies and I'll be responsible for seeing and writing about every single thing that gets a theatrical release, from big-budget shitheaps to tiny Turkish art films. It's a full-time position and yet I'm still allowed to continue writing about music for the other magazines I contribute to, provided I can make it all fit in my day.*

"Sorry if that ruins your dreams of being a male prostitute," says Morocco.

"I'll just start charging you," I say.

2. *Three days before my Brittany Murphy interview, an oozing, volcanic Krakatoa-level cold sore erupts on my lip.*

SCAB

IT FREAKS ME that people now use the prefix "herp" in relation to cold sores, one of which I currently own on my otherwise adorable face. I know that a cold sore is, in fact, a form of herpes, but I seem to recall never hearing that news as a child. They've popped up on my lips from time to time since I was a completely innocent first-grader, and no one looks at a kid with a cold sore and accuses him of making out with a herpes sufferer. If you're all grown up, however, people can't wait to lift an eyebrow. "Who were you fucking?" asks Dave 2.

"Your mom," I say, "And next time she's not getting a tip."

So I put goopy medicine on it and hide inside as much as I can, hoping it will subside to a manageable scab by the time I go face-to-face with the actress. It doesn't really work all that well.

Brittany Murphy is eating my Milky Way bar. We're sitting together on a foot-high cement block fence in a sun-beaten, ant-covered parking lot. She's still wearing the terrifyingly expensive cleavage-announcement dress she had on for the photo shoot she just finished. Not knowing when the photo shoot would wrap up, I showed up mid-morning and sat on a couch all day and watched her vamp inside a car and out, looking fake-afraid behind the wheel and draping herself across its hood, singing along loudly to a Rolling Stones CD. If I were a real journalist I'd have brought the candy as an ice-breaker and a way to frame the story: Wow, Brittany Murphy is so normal she'll eat the candy bar you offer. But I really brought the candy for myself because I didn't know how long I'd be waiting. Good thing the photo studio people provided food for me, the photographer, stylists, wardrobe-bringers, make-up and hair people, and a couple of other folks whose functions I couldn't quite figure out. I was able to save the candy bar for last, thanks to that, and thought sharing would just be the nice thing to do.

"Hey, Brittany, want a candy bar?"

"Ooh, what kind?

"Dark Chocolate Milky Way."

"Yes!"

After we settle down for the interview, my first question is, "So what do you think of my cold sore?"

"It doesn't really look like one," she says, "Usually they're all puffy and wet. It looks like a skateboarding accident. That's what you should tell people."

She may well be the most excitedly happy person I've met since moving here. She's the kind of girl you knew in high school who'd purposely squirt milk out of her nose in a restaurant just to make you scream laughing. Then you'd both get kicked out. Does this sound like a celebrity profile? Fuck, it does. Anyway, she's pretty adorable and it doesn't seem like a con. I get the idea from having watched her all day that she's like this with everyone. We chat about the shoot for a while. Then she asks me how I like Los Angeles.

"I hate it. Everyone drives me crazy. Every*thing* drives me crazy." I tell her about Gay Voice Publicist with Hepatitis

Shades and Teen Girl in the parking lot box. I can feel my heart start racing all over again as I tell it. When I'm finished, I say, "And I just miss Texas and I miss my friends and there are days when I just think everyone here is evil. Well, not you and my boyfriend. But the rest of these assholes, definitely."

"Yeah, well, they have evil people in Texas too, right? Lots of them, I'm sure. All those accountants. There are bad people everywhere you go, Dave." She's telling me in the most gentle, foxy, tits-up elementary-school-teacher manner ever. That's when I have an Oh Shit thought. I just got taught a fucking *life lesson* by a twentysomething celebrity millionaire. Worst of all, she's right. Furthermore, I just got a full-time writing job. I have so much work looming I'll have to start turning down the extra assignments that are merely guilty of not tickling my fancy. It makes no sense for me to still be this tightly wound. When we part, she gives me a big kiss on the cheek. "No, no no. Watch out. You'll get my cold sore," I say.

"It's a skateboarding accident," she replies.

In an effort to smooth out my shards-of-glass nerves, Morocco Mole takes me the Los Angeles County Museum of Art. We hit the Tar Pits first, of course, then wait outside for friends to show up so we can all go see *Boom!*, one of our favorite old movies. In this film, Elizabeth Taylor and Richard Burton recite head-scratchingly arty dialogue by Tennessee Williams to each other on a Mediterranean Island. Liz coughs up blood and wears sea-shell headdresses. Noël Coward drops by to talk about how women smell like fish. Dick stares at the ocean and says "boom" a lot. Then Liz drops dead. It's pretty awesome.

And suddenly Parker Posey is standing in front of me, smoking a cigarette. Yes, *that* Parker Posey. She's a friend of

Actor Craig's and boom, there she is, joining us for the movie. That's two celebrities in one day, right up in my personal space. I make small talk with the charming actor lady and resist telling her I paid good money to see *You've Got Mail* just because she was in it and that Tom Hanks and Meg Ryan now owe me ten bucks.

"Oh, you're new to L.A.?"

"Yeah. Been here a year now."

"Oh, so you're all settled then."

"No."

And why I then start in on the same tedious rant I always puke up is beyond me. It's a reflex. A stupid, stupid knee-jerk reaction. Meanwhile another thought pile-up chaotically assembles itself in my brain. I'm telling her about how I hate this city, how it's full of yuck and ick and ugh and how I'm "not from here, not one of them, not having it, and blah blah motherfuckin' blah." I don't even hear my own words anymore because, at the same time, inside, Gay Voice Hepatitis Shade-Wearing Publicist Who Should Be in Jail for Assault is screaming at me: "I'm an asshole but so are you, Dave White. *You* broke down and gave in to L.A. evil and became part of the machine you think you're so much better than. You spend your days at publicity junkets with people like me. We're colleagues. We're the same. So welcome to *my* town now. You're one of us and there's nothing you can do about it. You *chose* to be here. And you could have left anytime you wanted, you could have clicked your stupid little out-of-fashion Doc Martens three times and gone back to the hick state you claim you love so much. And really, fag—and you are a fag, just like all the other fags you think you're superior to—if you love your backward-ass home state so much then why don't you fucking marry it and take the redneck train home? You know why? Because you're staying. You're trapped. You have an enviable new career that you know you'd be an idiot to quit because it will eventually lead to some other soul-suck writing gig and you have people who love you in spite of yourself, you fucking ingrate. The truth is that this is what you wanted and now you've got it. And oh yeah, next? Like it or not? You're buying a cell phone."

I finish my boring mini-rant. Parker Posey stares at me. She takes a puff on her cigarette. "Oh really," she says, as deadpan as Sister Betty's flat-lining of the Magnetic Fields concert creep, and her exhalation fills my face with her smoke. "Well, it's a big city. What did you expect?" To have added "you big baby" to the end of her sentence would have been unnecessarily redundant.

Then she walks away to talk to someone else.

That's two bitch-slaps in one day. Two I deserve, even. Why is the universe sending me actresses and publicists dispensing Shut-Up-Dave-White wisdom? How is it that in less than twenty-four hours I've been schooled by both the *Party Girl* and the other *Girl, Interrupted* girl?

I'm quiet on the drive home up Crescent Heights toward the base of the Hollywood Hills where we live. A billion sparkly Los Angeles lights laid out in front of us. Morocco Mole says, "That was a surprise that Craig brought Parker Posey with him. I didn't know they knew each other. Did you talk to her?"

"A little."

"About...?"

"About 'How I'm Adjusting to Life in West Hollywood.'"

"Oh, that."

"Yeah."

"What did she say?"

I pause a second. Because I think I'm through. It's finally enough.

"She told me to get over it and quit whining like a little bitch."

"She said *that?*"

"In so many words, yes."

"Well," he turns his head and offers, gently, not in the playfully antagonistic way we've perfected as a long-term couple, "maybe you should."

Maybe I will.

Other stuff that happens:
1. *I stay.*

AFTER - 2006

IFILM LAID EVERYONE off when the dot-com boom went boom. *Glue* magazine went under too. *Glue* Laurie now works for a dot-com and I feed her celebrity spotting moments when I have good ones. It's a stupid sport but I still play it. Rick James and Ann Miller died. The mean transgender women moved out of my apartment building. So did hot Justin and the Woooo Girls. Now these two straight guys live under us. They watch a lot of football and don't seem to mind gay sex noises. Angry Parking Space Woman still lives in the building and spent several months battling some lesbian tenants over the parking space, eventually taking them on one of those sassy judge shows to fake-sue them. Ryan O'Neal went back to Malibu. The cape-wearing guy disappeared, as did the masturbating guy. The shirtless drug dealer still hangs out. HeteRobert got married to a woman, like straight people do. Sean and Vinny broke up—they both have new boyfriends now but they're still best friends, which isn't how straight people usually do it at all. Then Vinny moved away to New York. So did Maryam. Dave 2 is still super horny and would probably have sex with you. Spiritual Andy is on a TV show now where he talks about movies but he likes all the ones I think are shit. They tore down Jayne Mansfield's house. I never saw the Hep Shades Assault Publicist again. I did see Shelley Winters at Silver Spoon, but only once. My mother's smoking and high blood pressure caught up with her and she had a stroke. She lives in a nursing home now and has lost her ability to speak, so she can't sass back anymore. I fly home to Texas to visit her every couple of months and we see movies like *March of the Penguins.* Old people love that shit. And after about a week in Texas, I'm ready to come back to my other home. Finally, Morocco Mole is still my domestic partner. We got even fatter. We just had our ten-year anniversary. We still live in the same West Hollywood apartment because we're still the wrong kind of writers, the Not TV or Movie Kind who will never be able to afford a house in Los Angeles, a city that's bad and beautiful. The way I like it.